STUDENT STUDY GUIDE

FOR

GARGIULO'S

SPECIAL EDUCATION IN CONTEMPORARY SOCIETY
AN INTRODUCTION TO EXCEPTIONALITY

Harold C. Griffin
East Carolina University

Linda W. Griffin
Roanoke Chowan Community College

THOMSON

WADSWORTH

Australia • Canada • Mexico • Singapore • Spain • United Kingdom • United States

Printed in the United States of America

1 2 3 4 5 6 7   05 04 03 02 01

ISBN 0-534-57495-5

For more information about our products, contact us at:
Thomson Learning Academic Resource Center
1-800-423-0563

For permission to use material from this text, contact us by:
Phone: 1-800-730-2214
Fax: 1-800-731-2215
Web: www.thomsonrights.com

Asia
Thomson Learning
60 Albert Complex, #15-01
Albert Complex
Singapore 189969

Australia
Nelson Thomson Learning
102 Dodds Street
South Street
South Melbourne, Victoria 3205
Australia

Canada
Nelson Thomson Learning
1120 Birchmount Road
Toronto, Ontario M1K 5G4
Canada

Europe/Middle East/South Africa
Thomson Learning
Berkshire House
168-173 High Holborn
London WC1 V7AA
United Kingdom

Latin America
Thomson Learning
Seneca, 53
Colonia Polanco
11560 Mexico D.F.
Mexico

Spain
Paraninfo Thomson Learning
Calle/Magallanes, 25
28015 Madrid, Spain

CONTENTS

PREFACE

This Study Guide is designed to assist you in your exploration of *Special Education in Contemporary Society* by Richard Gargiulo. The Guide will stress important points made in each chapter as well as provide thought-provoking questions related to current trends and issues in the education of students with disabilities.

Each chapter of the study guide contains the following information:

1. **Chapter review** summarizes the focus of the chapter.
2. **Key Points** of the chapter highlight the most significant points.
3. **Focus and Reflect Questions** complement the chapter with thought-provoking questions regarding chapter content.
4. **Chapter Guided Review** provides a detailed outline of the chapter.
5. **Application Exercises and Project Suggestions** contain two parts:
    a. application exercises which enrich your understanding of the chapter content by utilizing interview and observation techniques
    b. InfoTrac® activities and article suggestions that complement the chapter being reviewed
6. **Key Terms** for each chapter are listed.
7. **Practice Test** consists of true/false, multiple-choice questions along with matching activities.

At the end of each practice test you will find an **Answer Key** for the test and an **Answer Key** for the **"Check your Understanding"** questions found in your textbook.

Special education has experienced vast changes in the past 30 years. The field has been shaped by legislation that has moved students with disabilities from segregated settings to inclusive classrooms. In addition, special education has been molded by new technologies, family involvement and ever-expanding views of disabilities. Along with all of the changes come new challenges for classroom teachers concerning students with disabilities. Your textbook along with your study guide will assist you in meeting these challenges and in expanding your understanding of exceptional students.

Harold C. Griffin
Linda W. Griffin

CHAPTER ONE
SPECIAL EDUCATION IN CONTEXT

Overview of Special Education in Context

Chapter One is an introduction to the study of special education. The author emphasizes the similarities between individuals with disabilities and typically developing individuals are more important than the differences. The chapter lays the foundation for further study by defining terms, outlining the history of special education, applying the ecological perspective to special education, and describing approaches of delivering instruction to exceptional learners.

Chapter One Key Points

- Special education is a study of human similarities and human differences.
- Educators must focus attention to the strengths and abilities of individual learners, not on their disabilities.
- The terms disability and handicap should not be used interchangeably.
- A disability is an inability or incapacity to perform a particular task in a specific way.
- A handicap describes the impact or consequence of the disability on the person.
- The foundations of special education began with eighteenth and nineteenth century European reformers.
- Collaboration between all professionals serving students with special needs has been recognized as an efficient means of delivering services.
- Individuals with disabilities have needs which span a lifetime.

Focus and Reflect

Discuss the term " developmentally delayed", noting advantages of using this broad terminology.

_____

_____

_____

Discuss the concept of special education.

_____

_____

_____

Describe the development of special education in public schools in America.

_____

_____

_____

Discuss the need for professional collaboration relating it to the learner with special needs.

_____

_____

_____

Chapter Guided Review

1. Exceptionality can be defined as a deviation from societal or community standards for normalcy.

2. The educational needs for some exceptional children can be met in general education classes by inclusive instruction.

3. The terms disability and handicap are not interchangeable. A disability is a limitation imposed on an individual that interferes with their ability to perform a task. A handicap is the impact the disability has on the individual as they try to interact with the environment.

4. Special education is an individualized instructional program, which meets the needs of learners who cannot be fully accommodated in the regular classroom.

5. By using the broad term "developmentally delayed", young children are able to receive special education services without the detrimental effects of being labeled.

6. The Individuals with Disabilities Education Act (IDEA) identifies thirteen categories of disability.

7. Individual states utilize the federal definition to determine who is eligible to receive special education services.

8. Gifted and talented students are not listed as a separate category in IDEA although any states provide special education services for these students.

9. Labeling students is stigmatizing, but it allows for special education services.

10. Determining prevalence figures for individuals with disabilities is affected by many factors:
    a. Identification and assessment measures
    b. Definitions of disabilities, which vary state to state
    c. Changing regulations regarding who is eligible for services

11. Learning disabilities has been the most rapidly growing area in special education.

12. European reformers laid the groundwork for today's view of special education as early as the late 1700's.

13. Many notable practitioners influenced the development of services for individuals with disabilities:
    a. Itard - "The Father of Special Education"
    b. Edouard Seguin - brought ideas of the importance of sensorimotor activities to the United States
    c. Gallaudet - established educational facilities for individuals who are deaf

14. Within the last thirty years, special education has grown from excluded, self-contained classrooms to inclusive classrooms.

15. Collaboration among professionals serving individuals with disabilities has given rise to several models:
    a. Consultative services
    b. Cooperative teaching
    c. Service delivery teams

16. Special education services may span throughout life with special emphasis on early childhood special education and transition services leading to vocational placements.

Application Exercises & Project Suggestions

1. Observe an inclusive classroom. List the modifications you observe being made for students with disabilities.
2. Interview an individual with a disability. Ask the individual in what ways (if any) the disability has been a handicap to them.
3. Discuss with a special education teacher some alternatives to the practice of labeling students in order for them to receive special education services.

InfoTrac® Activity Suggestions

Activity 1.1: Inclusive Practices
This activity is based on an article that lists several exceptional examples of inclusive practice. The article provides an insightful look at schools and educators who "get it" in regard to individuals with disabilities.

1. Locate and read the first five pages of "Models of Excellence in Education" found in *Exceptional Parent*.

2. Compare the Schnell Elementary School and the Phoenicia Elementary School. List the strengths of both programs.

----

3. Write one mission statement that describes the underlying philosophy of both schools.

----

4. Locate in the article the nomination for West Lyon Community School. How does the "Snack Pack" provide transitioning skills for these high school students?

Activity 1.2: Supplementary Aids and Services
This activity is based on an article that addresses the debate over determining supplementary aids and services for students with disabilities.

1. Locate and read "The IDEA Amendments: A four-Step Approach for Determining Supplementary Aids and Services" by Susan K Etscheidt and Larry Bartlett.

2. Contrast the terms "supplementary aids and services" and "related services".

_____

_____

_____

3. Describe the four dimensions that should be considered by an IEP team.

_____

_____

_____

InfoTrac® Article Suggestions
- Ruppert, E. (1998). The role of the pediatrician in the IEP or IFSP. The Exceptional Parent, 28, 72.
- Glelzheiser, M., McLane, M., Meyers, J., Pruzek, R. (1998). IEP-specified peer interaction needs: accurate but ignored. Exceptional Children, 65,51.

Key Terms
Define each:

Exceptional children _____

Disability _____

Handicap_____

Developmental delay_____

At-risk_____

Special education _____

Related services _____

Category_____

Noncategorical _____

Incidence_____

Prevalence_____

Self-contained_____

Ecology _____

Microsystem _____

Mesosystem _____

Exosystem _____

Macrosystem _____

Collaboration_____

Individualized Education Plan (IEP) _____

Consultation _____

Cooperative teaching _____

Multidisciplinary _____

Interdisciplinary _____

Transdisciplinary _____

Individualized family service plan (IFSP) _____

Early intervention _____

Early childhood special education _____

Transition _____

Transition services_____

Individualized transition plan (ITP)_____

CHAPTER ONE: SPECIAL EDUCATION IN CONTEXT
Practice Test

True or False

1. Gifted and talented students are classified in a separate category under IDEA. _____

2. A disability is not necessarily a handicap. _____

3. The most rapidly growing area of special education is mental retardation. _____

4. Authorities agree the practice of labeling students is the most effective method of providing services. _____

5. Itard is called the "Father of Special Education" due to his use of behavior modification techniques with a boy named Victor. _____

6. The terms "developmentally delayed" and "at-risk" can be used interchangeably. _____

7. The first special education classrooms were self-contained with pupils segregated from the rest of the students in the school. _____

8. The ecological perspective views the child in isolation not influenced by environment. _____

9. PL 94-142 mandated the multidisciplinary model in collaboration of services for students with disabilities. _____

10. The transdisciplinary model provides the most collaborative effort in delivering services to students with disabilities. _____

Multiple Choice

1. The most integrated intervention setting for exceptional learners is
   a. the resource room
   b. a special classroom
   c. the regular classroom
   d. a residential school

2. The most segregated level of intervention for exceptional learners is
   a. the resource room
   b. the regular classroom
   c. a residential school
   d. a special classroom

3. Which of the following special education pioneers was the founder of the American School for the Deaf?
   a. Seguin
   b. Itard
   c. Montessori
   d. Gallaudet

4. From an ecological perspective, a student's behavior is viewed as
    a. an interaction of person and environment
    b. no interaction between person and environment
    c. one student in isolation from all social context

5. The most rapidly growing area of special education is
    a. visually impaired
    b. mentally retarded
    c. learning disabled
    d. autism

6. Which of the following can be seen as a problem with labeling students by their exceptionalities?
    a. Labels can effect self-esteem.
    b. The label often becomes the person.
    c. Labels are stigmatizing.
    d. All of the above.

Matching

Incidence	Special Education
Category	Individual Transition Plan
Exceptional children	At-risk
Early Childhood Special Education	Cooperative teaching

1. The _____ links the school system and employment opportunities for the student.

2. _____ differ from societal and community standards for normalcy.

3. Harmful biological, environmental or genetic conditions can lead to a child being

    _____.

4. _____ is an individualized instruction program designed to meet the learner's needs.

5. Sharing common characteristics and features places individuals into a _____.

6. _____ refers to the number of new instances of a disability occurring with in a time period.

7. In _____ regular educators and special educators work together to provide services to a heterogeneous group.

8. _____ customized services for children with disabilities between 3-5 years of age.

Chapter 1: Special Education in Context
Practice Test Answer Key

True or False
1. False. Gifted and talented is not a category under IDEA.
2. True.
3. False. Learning disabilities is the most rapidly growing area in special education.
4. False. There is much disagreement among authorities over labeling students for provision of services.
5. True.
6. False. Developmentally delayed is a disability; at-risk indicates that the conditions exist which could cause an individual to be disabled.
7. True.
8. False. The ecological perspective views the child as being constantly influenced by his environment.
9. True.
10. True.

Multiple Choice
1. C
2. C
3. D
4. A
5. C
6. D

Matching
1. Individual Transition Plan
2. Exceptional children
3. at-risk
4. Special education
5. category
6. Incidence
7. cooperative teaching
8. Early Childhood Special Education

Check Your Understanding ⇨**See textbook page 37**
Answer Key

1. **How is the concept of normalcy related to the definition of children identified as exceptional?**
Normalcy is a concept determined by reference group and certain circumstances. An individual is judged as exceptional upon the group's criteria of normalcy.

2. **Differentiate between the terms disability and handicap. Provide specific examples of each term.**
A disability is a limitation imposed on an individual by loss or reduction in functioning. A handicap refers to the problems the disability causes for the individual in functioning within the environment. Being in a wheelchair would be a handicap for someone in a building without an elevator, but would not be a handicap for that person while sitting in the classroom.

3. **What is special education?**
Special education is a customized instructional program designed to meet the unique needs of the learner.

4. **Name the thirteen categories of exceptionality presently recognized by the federal government.**
Autism, deaf-blindness, hearing impairments, mental retardation, multiple disabilities, orthopedic impairments, emotional disturbance, specific learning disabilities, speech or language impairments, traumatic brain injury, visual impairments, developmental delay and other health impairments.

5. **Compare and contrast arguments for and against the practice of labeling pupils according to their disability.**
Although labels can be stigmatizing, they serve as a means for funding and establishing an individual's eligibility for services. Labels can affect self-concept as well as lowering expectations of the individual. Labels allow professionals to communicate efficiently about services for the individual.

6. **How are the terms prevalence and incidence used when discussing individuals with disabilities?**
Incidence is the number of new instances of a disability occurring within a given time frame. Prevalence refers to the total number of individuals with a particular disability currently existing in a population at a given time.

7. **Identify contributing factors to the growth of the field of special education.**
The passage of PL 99-457 has increased the number of infants and toddlers served in special education. The population of students identified as learning disabled has jumped since the passage of PL 94-142.

8. **Why do you think the federal government has not mandated special education for students who are gifted and talented?**
Students who are gifted and talented are not recognized under IDEA.

9. **What role did Europeans play in the development of special education in the US?**
European reformers laid the groundwork for today's special education. Students of the reformers immigrated to the United States bringing European ideas with them. Americans traveled to Europe to be trained and return to the United States.

10. **According to Bronfenbrenner's ecological model, how should special educators view students with disabilities and their families?**

Students with disabilities and their families are seen as part of a social scheme whereby they influence and are influenced by the various environments and settings they encounter.

11. **What are related services, and why are they important for the delivery of a special education?**

Related services are any services needed by the individual that will help them achieve their educational potential. Many children need a wide range of services related to their specific disability.

12. **How can cooperative teaching benefit students with and without disabilities?**

When the regular educator and the special educator worki together in cooperative teaching, all students benefit from the specialties of both.

13. **List the characteristics that distinguish multidisciplinary, interdisciplinary, and transdisciplinary educational teams. What are the advantages and disadvantages of each teaming model?**

In the multidisciplinary team model, each professional performs their duty independent of the other team members. In the interdisciplinary model, professionals work independently yet collaborate on their findings to produce a more holistic approach to treatment. In the transdisciplinary model, the professionals conduct their evaluations then work with one team leader who provides the interventions necessary. The multidisciplinary model is the least collaborative of the models while the transdisciplinary model is the most collaborative. The transdisciplinary model also calls for the most family involvement of the three models.

14. **How does this author define the term *early intervention*? What is its purpose?**

The author sees early intervention as a "whole child" approach that encompasses children and their families from birth through age 5. This approach includes not only educational services but also health and family support services.

15. **Why is transitioning important for students with disabilities at the secondary level?**

Transition is important in order to assure the secondary level student has clear objectives and goals for the next phase in their life.

16. **What challenges do professionals face as they prepare adolescents to move from school to adult life in the community?**

The transition curriculum must include all facets of adult life, including work behaviors as well as social skill behaviors and personal time management behaviors. All students need these skills. Some students, however, will need to have these skills taught in direct instruction. Balancing the rigors of academic life as well as social training is the challenge for professionals.

CHAPTER TWO
POLICIES, PRACTICES, AND PROGRAMS

Overview of Policies, Practices, and Programs

A barrage of court cases and federal legislation has shaped our present day practices in special education. Chapter Two discusses some of the key litigations and federal laws that govern the delivery of services to individuals with disabilities. The author examines the assessment and referral process along with interpretations applied to the concept of least restrictive environment.

Chapter Key Points

- Securing the right to a free, appropriate public education for students with disabilities was a difficult process involving many court cases that led to federal legislation.
- PL 94-142, the Education for All Handicapped Children Act, was the first law to guarantee a public education to all children.
- PL 94-142 was renamed in 1990 to the Individuals with Disabilities Education Act (IDEA).
- Proper assessment leads to correct identification and placement for special education services.
- Each student aged 3-21 receiving special education services has an individualized education program (IEP) to guide the scope of their instructional plan.
- Placing students in the least restrictive environment has lead to many concepts including mainstreaming and full inclusion.

Focus and Reflect

1. Discuss the provisions of PL 99-457.

_____

_____

_____

2. Discuss the importance of using formal and informal means of assessment.

_____

_____

_____

3. Outline the special education placement process beginning with pre-referral interventions through least restrictive setting placements. Include in your outline the timelines for IEP development and evaluation.

_____

_____

_____

_____

_____

Chapter Guided Review

1. The landmark case of Brown v. Board of Education of Topeka set the precedent for many of the litigations that led to legislation for children with disabilities.

2. From the 1970's through the 1990's, several key pieces of federal legislation have been enacted for individuals with disabilities.

3. PL 94-142, the Education for All Handicapped Children Act was signed in 1975.
   a. Free appropriate public education
   b. Least restrictive environment
   c. Individualized Education Program
   d. Procedural due process
   e. Non-discriminatory assessment
   f. Parent participation

4. PL 99-457 (Amendments to PL 94-142) extended services for young children
   a. Included children 3-5 years of age in free, appropriate public education
   b. Title I created the Handicapped Infant and Toddlers Program

5. PL 101-476 renamed PL 94-142 to the Individuals with Disabilities Education Act in 1990.
   a. expanded services
   b. autism and traumatic brain injury added as categories

6. Americans with Disabilities Act (ADA) passed in 1990.
   a. guarantees civil rights to anyone who has any type of impairment
   b. requires public establishments to provide accommodations for people with impairments

7. PL 105-17 amended IDEA in 1997.
   a. addressed discipline of students with disabilities
   b. regular educators are included on IEP teams
   c. revision was made on some definitions

8. Interindividual differences are differences between students.

9. Intraindividual differences are differences within the individual that manifest as the person's strengths and weaknesses.

10. Referral and proper assessment result in proper placement
    a. prereferral interventions need to be utilized
    b. the referral is a request for evaluation
    c. assessment by a multidisciplinary team is the next step
    d. identification for services

11. Individualized Education Programs (IEPs) are developed after eligibility has been established.
    a. present level of functioning
    b. short-term and long-term goals established
    c. collaboration of regular and special educators

12. Individualized Family Service Plans (IFSPs) are developed for young children.

13. The concept of least restrictive environment governs the location of the provision of special education services.

14. Mainstreaming and full inclusion are outcomes of the controversy over least restrictive environment.

Application Exercises & Project Suggestions

1. Interview parents of a student with disabilities. Discuss the parents' reaction to the concept of full inclusion.

2. Discuss with a regular educator the new requirements of IDEA that mandate more involvement of regular educators in the IEP planning process.

3. Visit an early intervention program. Following the visit, produce a brochure for the program outlining the benefits of early intervention.

InfoTrac® Activity Suggestions

Activity 2.1: Inclusion
This article addresses the ways first-year teachers can meet the requirement of including special needs students in the classroom. The author provides suggestions on ways to make the special needs student feel like a part of the community in the classroom.

1. Locate and read " **Inclusion: What Can Teachers Do?**" by Joe Stahl.

2. Describe three strategies the author suggests to welcome the special needs student in the classroom.

_____

_____

_____

3. List two teaching strategies that can be employed to aid the special needs student.

_____

_____

_____

4. After reading the article, what types of grading procedures would you use with the special needs students?

_____

_____

_____

Activity 2.2: Mainstreaming
This article deals with attitudes of regular and special educators toward mainstreaming. Factors such as implementation of different instructional strategies for students with disabilities were examined.

1.Locate and read pages 1 and 2 of **"Are Attitudes and Practices Regarding Mainstreaming Changing? A Case of Teachers in Two Rural School Districts"** by Yona Leyser and Kara Tappendorf.

2. What two factors seem to help develop positive attitudes toward mainstreaming?

_____

_____

_____

3. List four elements that influence the teacher's use of adaptations and accommodations for students with special needs.

_____

_____

InfoTrac® Article Suggestions
- Milone, M. (2000). Special teachers for special needs. <u>Technology and Learning,</u> <u>20</u>, 40.
- Fuchs, D., & Fuchs, L. (1998). Competing visions for educating students with disabilities: inclusion versus full inclusion. <u>Childhood Education,</u> <u>74</u>, 317-321.

Key Terms
Define each:

Interindividual differences_____

Intraindividual differences_____

Prereferral intervention_____

Referral _____

Child-find_____

Assessment _____

Multidisciplinary team _____

Norm-referenced_____

Criterion-referenced_____

Individualized education program (IEP) _____

Individualized family service plan (IFSP)_____

Least restrictive environment _____

Mainstreaming _____

Regular education initiative _____

Full inclusion_____

CHAPTER TWO: POLICIES, PRACTICES, AND PROGRAMS
Practice Test

True or False

1. Mainstreaming is a written mandate in the first law passed for the education of handicapped children. _____

2. The concept of a continuum of educational services is relatively new to the field of special education. _____

3. PL 94-142 was the first public law mandating a free, appropriate public education for all children with disabilities. _____

4. Special educators are in agreement concerning the degree of integration needed for each student with disabilities. _____

5. The concept of the Regular Education Initiative called for greater collaboration between regular and special educators. _____

6. The least restrictive setting for one student with a disability may be highly restrictive to another student with disabilities. _____

7. The American with Disabilities Act created a provision for the Handicapped Infant and Toddlers Program. _____

8. PL 94-142 was renamed in 1990 to the Individuals with Disabilities Education Act.

   _____

9. PL 94-142 mandated a standard form to be used for all IEPs._____

10. Norm-referenced tests compare a student's performance with the performance of other students of the same age. _____.

11. There is equal sharing of the cost of educating students with special needs between state and federal governments. _____

Multiple Choice

1. The rights of individuals with disabilities to nondiscriminatory treatment in the workplace, transportation, public services and state and local governments was guaranteed by
   a. IDEA
   b. PL 99-457
   c. ADA
   d. PL 94-142

2. An Individualized Education Program must include:
   a. present level of functioning
   b. short-term and long-term goals
   c. a statement of special education services, related services and supplementary aids
   d. all of the above

3. The concept of full inclusion stresses that
   a. special education students are segregated from the rest of the school population
   b. special education students are included in the regular education class for part of the school day
   c. special education students are educated completely in the regular education classroom

4. When was PL 94-142, the Education for All Handicapped Children Act, passed?
   a. 1960
   b. 1990
   c. 1975
   d. 1997

5. According to the new amendments for IDEA, the category of developmentally delayed may be used for
   a. children, birth to 5
   b. children, birth to 3
   c. children aged 3 to 9
   d. children aged 3 to 21

6. The pre-referral interventions:
   a. help to reduce unwarranted referrals to special education.
   b. stimulate a collaboration between regular and special education teachers.
   c. are preemptive in design.
   d. all of the above.

7. IDEA mandates an IFSP for infants and toddlers receiving special education services. When must the IFSP be developed?
   a. within 30 days after referral for services has been made
   b. within 6 months after referral for services has been made
   c. within 45 days after referral for services has been made
   d. none of the above

Matching

Intraindividual	Child-find
Referral	Individualized Education Program
Mainstreaming	PL 99-457
Full inclusion	Disabilities
Individual	Criterion-referenced assessments

1. _____ are differences within the individual.

2. _____ is a written request to evaluate a student to determine if the student has a disability.

3. _____ deal with intra-individual differences and are useful in planning instruction.

4. _____ is a strategy developed to deliver appropriate services to students ages 3 and older.

5. _____ is the belief that all children should be taught exclusively in general education classrooms.

6. The social and instructional integration of students with disabilities into educational programming whose purpose serves typically developing students is _____.

7. IDEA replaced the term "handicapped" with _____ and "children" with _____.

8. _____ mandated an IFSP for infants and toddlers with disabilities.

9. _____ services locate children who need to be screened and evaluated for special education services.

Chapter 2: Policies, Practices, And Programs
Practice Test Answer Key

True or False
1. False. Mainstreaming is not a written mandate in P.L. 94-142.
2. False. The concept of a continuum of educational services for children with disabilities has been in existence for over thirty years.
3. True
4. False. The degree of integration needed for each student varies because of the needs of the students. There is frequently disagreement concerning the level of integration that should occur.
5. True
6. True.
7. False. The Americans with Disabilities Act focused on the removal of barriers for individuals with disabilities. This included architectural, travel, and employment barriers.
8. True
9. False. P. L. 94-142 mandated components for the IEP but the IEP format was left up to states and districts to develop.
10. True
11. False. The federal government, state government, and local government all contribute to the costs of educating children with disabilities. The exact proportion which each contributes varies from year to year depending on appropriations.

Multiple Choice
1. C
2. D
3. C
4. C
5. C
6. D
7. C

Matching
1. intra-individual
2. referral
3. criterion-referenced assessments
4. individualized education program
5. full inclusion
6. mainstreaming
7. disabilities, individuals
8. P. L. 99-457
9. child-find

Check Your Understanding ⇨See textbook page 74
Answer Key

1. **How have litigation and legislation influenced the field of special education?**
Litigations have caused the courts to scrutinize public practices regarding individuals with disabilities that have led to legislation for these individuals.

2. **What is the significance of Brown vs. BOE, Pennsylvania Association for Retarded Children vs. Commonwealth of Pennsylvania, Larry P. vs. Riles, BOE vs. Rowley, and, Daniel R. R. vs. State BOE?**
- *Brown vs. Board of Education* set the groundwork against unlawful discrimination toward any group of individuals.
- *PARC vs. Commonwealth of Pennsylvania*: set the precedent of parental rights in decisions affecting the education of their children
- *Larry P. vs. Riles*: ruled against discriminatory testing of minority students
- *Daniel R. R. vs. State Board of Education*: provided a ruling on least restrictive environment for students with severe disabilities.

3. **Name and describe the six major components and guarantees contained in PL 94-142.**
- free, appropriate public education for all children regardless of the severity of their disability
- least restrictive environment where the child can, as much as possible, be educated with students without disabilities
- individualized education program describes an educational plan for each learner with disabilities
- procedural due process outlines parental rights in terms of their child's education
- nondiscriminatory assessment of children that is racially, culturally, or linguistically unbiased
- parental participation in the educational decision-making process

4. **How did PL 105-17 modify PL 101-476?**
P. L. 105-17 restructured P. L. 101-476 into four parts, revised some of the definitions, and revamped funding procedures as well as addressing the disciplining of students with disabilities.

5. **What was the purpose of the American with Disabilities Act? List four areas where this law affects the lives of individuals who are disabled.**
The ADA forbids discrimination against people with disabilities in public and private sectors of society. This laws affects individuals who are disabled in the workplace, on mass transit systems, hotels, and other public facilities, and in telecommunications services.

6. **Distinguish between interindividual and intraindividual differences.**
Inter-individual differences are differences between people, whereas intra-individual differences are within one person and manifest as strengths or weaknesses.

7. **How do prereferral interventions benefit the student suspected of requiring a special education?**
Pre-referral interventions aid in eliminating unnecessary referrals as well as providing individualized intervention for the student without the benefit of special education.

8. **How do norm-referenced and criterion-referenced tests differ?**
Norm-referenced tests compare the individual's performance with other students of the same age. A criterion-referenced test examines the individual's strengths and weakness

9. **List the key elements required of a meaningful IEP. Who is responsible for developing this document?**
    - student's present level of functioning
    - annual and short-term goals
    - special education, related services, and supplementary aids and services to be provided and level of integration for the student
    - explanation, if needed, of non-participation in the regular classroom
    - any individual modification needed for the student
    - projected date for initiation of services
    - transition planning
    - how progress will be measured

A multi-disciplinary team involving parents and professionals develops the IEP.

10. **Compare the provisions and purpose of an IFSP with those of an IEP**

The IFSP is designed to keep the family as primary caregivers emphasizing constant, active family involvement. The goals of the IFSP center around the concerns of the family.

11. **Define the following terms: mainstreaming, least restrictive environment, and regular education initiative. How are these terms related to the mandate of providing services in the LRE?**
    - Mainstreaming: the social and instructional integration of students with disabilities with educational programs for students without disabilities
    - Least restrictive environment: the concept that individuals with disabilities are to be educated in environments as close as possible to the general education classroom.
    - Regular Education Initiative: a partnership between general and special education that would result in coordination of the delivery of services.

The student with disabilities must have their least restrictive environment setting determined by collaboration between general and special education.

12. **Distinguish between a cascade of services delivery model and the philosophy of full inclusion. What do you see as the advantages and disadvantages of full inclusion?**

In the cascade of service delivery model, the individual can be placed in a hierarchy of educational environments according to the needs of the individual whereas in full inclusion the general education classroom is seen as the exclusive placement option for the student. Full inclusion calls for greater collaboration between all professionals working with students with disabilities. Students with disabilities will be able to participate as full-time members of the classroom.

CHAPTER THREE
CULTURAL AND LINGUISTIC DIVERSITY
AND EXCEPTIONALITY

Overview of Cultural and Linguistic Diversity and Exceptionality
This chapter examines the changing face of American society. The author examines factors that contribute to over- and under-representation of culturally and linguistically diverse students in special education programs.

Chapter Key Points
- The United States has moved from a "melting pot" concept concerning the influx of other cultures to a more accommodating view of cultural pluralism.
- Multicultural education and bilingual education present new challenges for both regular educators and special educators.
- The over-and under-representation of culturally diverse students in some categories of special education is affected by social, economic, cultural and political factors.
- Numerous assessment strategies need to be used for accurate assessment of the strengths and weaknesses of culturally and linguistically diverse students.
- Cultural awareness must be reflected in the formulation of IEPs for linguistically and cultural diverse students.

Focus and Reflect
Describe four areas in which special educators must focus attention in order to meet the requirements of culturally and linguistically diverse students.

_____

_____

_____

Discuss reasons why children from diverse cultures may experience difficulty in succeeding in American schools.

_____

_____

_____

What is your opinion of bilingual education? Do you feel bilingual education is success-oriented?

_____

_____

_____

Chapter Guided Review

1. The diversity of American society is presenting a challenge to American classrooms.

2. Cultural pluralism is replacing the idea of a "melting pot" society.
   a. multiculturalism advocates the ability to live in more than one culture
   b. multicultural education values the culture of each student
   c. bilingual education aids students who are not English proficient

3. Bilingual education serves as one alternative to aid students from linguistically diverse cultures to become successful in American schools.

4. Disproportional representation exists for minorities in some special education programs
   a. socioeconomic factors contribute, resulting in poor healthcare
   b. accurate testing for diverse cultures is needed
   c. insensitivity to learning styles is a contributing factor

5. Assessment measures need to be culturally sensitive
   a. standardized test bias promotes inaccurate identification
   b. a new definition, recognizing multiple intelligences, is expanding the view of intelligence
   c. portfolio assessments provide the student with more authentic assessment of strengths and weaknesses

6. Culturally sensitive curriculum programs offer the best promise of success for culturally and linguistically diverse students.

Application Exercises & Project Suggestions

1. Interview a senior adult from a different culture Ask them what changes have occurred in their culture in the last 30 years.
2. Interview a student in a bilingual education program. Ask them what improvements (if any) would they like to see implemented in the program.

InfoTrac® Article Suggestions

Activity 3.1: Community Colleges and the Hispanic Community
This article examines three areas of the country where community colleges are acting as valuable resources for the Hispanic communities in their areas.

1. Locate and read **"ESL and Beyond"** by Eleanor Lee Yates.

_____

_____

_____

2. Describe the services Santa Ana College is offering to aid Hispanics transition to college.

_____

_____

_____

3. Why has North Carolina experienced such growth in its Latino population?

_____

_____

_____

4. How is Durham Technical Community College helping Hispanic residents in the school and workplace environments?

_____

_____

_____

Activity 3.2: Bilingual Education
This article is an interview with Rosalie Porter, founder of the READ Institute, concerning her views about bilingual education.

1. Locate and read **"Porter Challenges Bilingual Education"** by Stephen Goode in ***Insight on the News***.
2. What reasons does Ms. Porter give for her opposition to bilingual education?

_____

_____

_____

3. How does she feel the program could be improved?

_____

_____

_____

InfoTrac® Article Suggestions
- Johannsen, K. (2001). Bridging the gap – Learning languages has taken a quantum leap as it enters the twenty-first century. World and I, 16, 120.
- Barone, M. (2000). In plain English. U.S. News and World Report, 128, 37.

Key Terms
Define each:

melting pot_____

cultural pluralism_____

culture_____

multiculturalism_____

multicultural education_____

bilingual education_____

ethnocentrism_____

macroculture_____

microcultures_____

limited English proficient (LEP)_____

bilingual special education_____

overrepresentation_____

underrepresentation_____

field dependent/sensitive_____

field independent_____

nondiscriminatory testing_____

multiple intelligence_____

portfolio assessment_____

CHAPTER THREE
CULTURAL AND LINGUISTIC DIVERSITY AND EXCEPTIONALITY
Practice Test

True or False

1. Culturally and linguistically diverse students are over-represented in all categories of special education._____

2. Ethnocentrism is an outcome of multicultural education. _____

3. American culture is a macroculture composed of microcultures._____

4. The primary purpose of bilingual education is to provide assistance to students with limited English proficiency so that they may function effectively in their native language and English. _____

5. A student can be eligible for special education services if the reason for their education difficulties is a limited proficiency of English._____

6. The information gathered from standardized tests is infallible._____

7. A new concept of intelligence has emerged which proposes a broader view of intelligence._____

8. The pupil's life experiences can be used as the building blocks for an authentic and culturally relevant curriculum._____

9. Portfolio assessment provides only a limited view of a student's performance._____

10. Teacher expectations are a contributing factor in the over- and under-representation of culturally and linguistically diverse students in special education programs._____

Multiple Choice

1. Contributing factors to the over-representation of minority groups in special education programs are
   a. poverty, faulty identification procedures, and teacher bias
   b. ethnic group identification, federal funding and teacher placement
   c. different value systems, politics, and ethnic group identification

2. The structure of American society is now likened to
   a. a melting pot
   b. a stereotypic environment
   c. a patchwork quilt
   d. an exclusive country club

3. The theory of multiple intelligences has been developed by
   a. Itard
   b. Gardner
   c. Kaufman
   d. Piaget

4. Factors that contribute to the under-representation of certain groups in gifted and talented programs are
        a. peer pressure not to excel in academics
        b. negative teacher perceptions of minority students
        c. lack of teacher training in the area of gifted and talented
        d. all of the above

5. Reasons for the changing demographics in the United States include
        a. greater immigration of non-European populations
        b. greater numbers of childbearing age women in non-white, non-Anglo ethnic groups
        c. higher birth rates among non-white, non-Anglo women
        d. all of the above

6. The traditional standardized test has been criticized for
        a. not being available in languages other than English.
        b. taking into account student culture and ethnic background.
        c. containing test bias which can influence results.
        d. a and c
        e. b and c

Matching

1. nondiscriminatory testing _____
2. microcultures   _____
3. ethnocentrism _____
4. portfolio assessment _____
5. macroculture   _____
6. bilingual special education _____
7. culture _____
8. field dependent/sensitive _____
9. field independent _____

    a. viewing one's own culture as being superior
    b. evaluation of student-gathered work samples
    c. the concept of a core national culture
    d. attitudes, values and belief systems shared by a particular group of people
    e. approaching learning intuitively
    f. subcultures
    g. uses the student's home language and culture as the foundation to build appropriate education
    h. non-biased evaluation procedures
    i. detail-oriented and analytical

Chapter 3: Cultural and Linguistic Diversity and Exceptionality
Practice Test Answer Key

True or False
1. False. Culturally and linguistically diverse students are under-represented in programs for gifted and talented students.
2. False. Cultural pluralism is an outcome of multicultural education.
3. True.
4. True.
5. False. Limited English proficiency cannot be a reason for eligibility.
6. False. The information gathered from standardized tests is often questioned.
7. True.
8. True.
9. False. Portfolio assessments provide a broad view of a student's strengths and weaknesses.
10. True.

Multiple Choice
1. a
2. c
3. b
4. d
5. d
6. d

Matching
1. h
2. f
3. a
4. b
5. c
6. g
7. d
8. e
9. i

Check Your Understanding ⇨See textbook page 105
Answer Key

1. **What do the terms culture and cultural diversity mean to you?**
(Answers will vary according to your interpretation.) Culture is the value systems, beliefs and traditions that form the heritage of a particular group of people. Cultural diversity incorporates the differences that make each culture unique.

2. **At one time, the US was described as a melting pot. Why? Metaphorically speaking, American society is now characterized as a floral bouquet or patchwork quilt. What factors contributed to this change in thinking?**
The United States was considered a "melting pot" due to the premise that cultures entering the United States would abandon their traditions and heritage, thus creating one "American" culture. In the 1960's, issues of civil rights and equal opportunities began to emerge as political and social issues that catalyzed scrutiny of different cultures.

3. **Define the following terms: cultural pluralism, multicultural education, and bilingual education.**

Cultural pluralism is a concept where cultural and ethnical differences are respected not admonished. Multicultural education values and respects the cultural background of each pupil in educational planning. Bilingual education is providing instruction to students, whose first language is not English, in their native language while they develop competency in English.

4. **Why is bilingual education a controversial topic?**

Bilingual education has caused controversy for many reasons: English has been declared the official language in some states, educators are undecided concerning proper transitioning time for bilingual students into the regular classroom, and research indicates that language may be acquired more quickly in informal settings.

5. **Compare and contrast the various instructional models used with students who are bilingual.**

Various programs are used for bilingual students: transitional programs are the most common model that uses the student's native language for academic instruction while infusing English instruction until the student is competent in English; the maintenance program model has a strong native language influence with little emphasis on leaving the program; the immersion program model uses English as the only language for instruction which results in a "sink or swim" philosophy; ESL programs use English proficiency as the primary goal with little use of the student's native language; sheltered English models use English for instruction and do not try to maintain any type or proficiency in the student's native language.

6. **Explain why pupils from minority groups experience disproportional representation in some special education programs.**

Some of the reasons for disproportional representation of minorities are inaccurate identification procedures combined with inappropriate assessment techniques such as test bias, teacher expectations, and bias and inconsistency in instructional methods.

7. **What are the consequences of disproportional representation?**

Disproportional representation can lead to unequal educational opportunities, underachievement and higher dropout risk.

8. **Why is the assessment of culturally and linguistically diverse students perceived to be problematic? How might these difficulties be corrected?**

The assessment process may be biased, as well as lack appropriate measurement tools. Assessment must be culturally sensitive.

9. **Define portfolio assessment. Identify the advantages of this strategy for evaluating the performance of children who are culturally and linguistically diverse.**

Portfolio assessment is an evaluation of authentic tasks performed by the student using various indicators gathered over a period of time. Portfolio assessment is outcome produced thus a true picture of a student's learning is represented in contrast to the one-time performance demonstrated on a standardized test.

CHAPTER FOUR
PARENTS, FAMILIES, AND EXCEPTIONALITY

Overview of Parents, Families, and Exceptionality
Chapter Four is an overview of the evolution of parent-professional collaboration. The author emphasizes the growth in this process. Also a family systems model and its components are discussed. Further, a stage theory model concerning parental reactions to the diagnosis of a disability is explained.

Chapter Key Points
- The eugenics movement laid the foundation that parents were the cause of their child's disability.
- Professionals serve the families rather than just the parents of children with disabilities.
- Turnbull and Turnbull's Family Systems Model includes family characteristics, family interactions, family functions, and life cycle changes.
- The stage theory model for explaining parental reactions to the diagnosis of a disability stresses the primary, secondary, and tertiary phases of reactions.
- To develop meaningful relationships with parents, professionals must exhibit honesty, trust, respect, genuine caring, active listening, and a respect for the family's cultural differences and beliefs.

Focus and Reflect
1. Discuss the meaning of collaboration.

_____

_____

_____

2. Discuss the three phases of the stage model of parental reactions to their child's disability.

_____

_____

_____

3. Discuss the concept of transitions as part of the family life cycle.

_____

_____

_____

4. Discuss the impact of a child with disabilities on the marital relationship of the parents.

_____

_____

_____

Chapter Guided Review

1. Parent-professional relationships: changing roles
    a. antagonistic and adversarial relationships - eugenics movement (sterilization to reduce number of unfit parents); refrigerator mothers of autistic children; often distrust between parents and professionals
    b. building working relationships - PL 94-142 - parents are active participants in educational decisions; services for the family not just the parents
    c. parent empowerment and family centered relationships-professionals and families collaborate; stresses power with families; ecological approach to family systems

2. A family systems approach
    a. family characteristics-family size, background, socioeconomic status, family health, challenges faced by family
    b. family interactions-cohesion and adaptability of the family
    c. adaptability-family's ability to change in response to crisis/stressful events
    d. family functions-affection, self-esteem, economics, daily care, socialization, recreation, and education
    e. family life cycle-developmental family changes over time; transitions; major life cycles stages include early childhood, school age, adolescence, and adulthood

3. The effects of a child's disability on parents and the family
    a. identification of a child as disabled affects entire family
    b. reactions of family member is subjective, personalized, and subject to individual interpretation of disability

4. Stages of parental reaction to disability
    a. primary phase-shock, denial grief, and depression
    b. secondary phase-ambivalence, guilt, anger, shame, and embarrassment
    c. tertiary phase-bargaining, adaptation/reorganization, acceptance and adjustment
    d. family adaptation to disability linked to support of family members and community resources

5. Disability and the family
    a. marital relations-frequently marital tension and stress in families of children with disabilities
    b. fathers of children with disabilities-less emotional response to disabilities, affected by visibility of disability, focuses on long-term consequences
    c. siblings of children with disabilities-response to disability (affected by socioeconomic status, family size, severity of disability, age spacing, sibling's gender); reactions to disabilities (depression, survivor's guilt, confusion, greater tolerance towards others, increased compassion, assistance for siblings (literature, support groups)
    d. grandparents of children with disabilities-go through stages of acceptance, can provide assistance to families, concerned about own child and grandchild

6. Working with families who are culturally and linguistically diverse
    a. roadblocks to involvement-limited English proficiency, unfamiliarity with rights, negative experiences with schools, deference to teachers as decision makers
    b. cultural sensitivity-awareness, respect and appreciation of values and perspectives of other cultures

7. Cultural reactions to disability
    a. disability-how child functions in home environment and family's expectations for child
    b. cause of disability-varies among cultures; God's will, intergenerational, reprisal factors, etc.

8. Suggestions for facilitating family and professional partnerships
    a. explain terminology to parents and professionals
    b. acknowledge feelings of parents
    c. actively listen to the parents
    d. use of two-step process when informing parents that their child requires special education services-give parents time to comprehend what they have been told; second meeting focus on intervention strategies
    e. keep parents informed-be positive; show respect, concern and desire to cooperate
    f. be accountable-follow through on agreements with families
    g. recognize diverse family structures and parenting styles-allow families the right to choose level of involvement

Application Exercises & Project Suggestions

1. Attend an IEP meeting. Discuss the roles of the parents and professionals who attended the meeting.
2. Attend a local council meeting of an advocacy group (United Cerebral Palsy, Association for Retarded Citizens, Parents Supporting Parents, etc.). Discuss two strategies the group uses to affirm the power of parents.
3. Interview a family of a child with disabilities. Discuss the rewards and challenges that these families experience on a daily basis.

InfoTrac® Activity Suggestions

Activity 4.1: Family life cycle
This activity is based on an article that discusses societal expectations of individuals with disabilities that often produce stigmatization for the individual with disabilities and their families.

1. Locate and read **"Disability and the Family Life Cycle"** published by Basic Books.

2. Discuss the concept of culturally licensed stigmatization.

_____
_____
_____

3. Discuss the idea that compensatory opportunities can be provided to cope with the constraints of a person's disability.

_____
_____
_____

4. Discuss the idea that non-disabled individuals also experience out of sync societal expectations.

_____
_____
_____

Activity 4.2: Cultural sensitivity

This article discusses the individual bias towards culturally appropriate beliefs and behavior, which everyone possesses.
1. Locate and read **"Cultural Sensitivity"** by Denise Bender found in ***Physical Therapy***.

2. Discuss why a person's personal beliefs, practices and needs should be considered during therapy treatment.

_____

_____

_____

3. Why is cultural sensitivity a difficult concept?

_____

_____

_____

4. How does cultural sensitivity assist in beneficial therapist-recipient interactions?

_____

_____

_____

InfoTrac Article Suggestions:
-   Khorazaty, M. (1997). Twentieth century family life cycle and its determinants in the United States. Journal of Family History, 22, 70-110.
-   Kelly, J. (1997). Changing issues in leisure-family research-again. Journal of Leisure Research, 29, 132-135.

Key Terms
Define each:

eugenics movement_____

family systems mode_____

family characteristics_____

family interaction_____

cohesion_____

adaptability_____

family functions_____

family life cycle_____

transitions_____

stage theory_____

cultural sensitivity_____

active listening _____

CHAPTER FOUR: PARENTS, FAMILIES, AND EXCEPTIONALITY
Practice Test

True or False

1. In working with children with disabilities, professionals work only with parents in collaborative relationships._____

2. The eugenics movement stressed sterilization to reduce the number of unfit parents and inferior offspring._____

3. Refrigerator moms were seen by Bettelheim as a cause of autism._____

4. Parents frequently were part of the collaborative educational planning process before the passage of P. L. 94-142._____

5. Family interactions include the concepts of cohesion and adaptability._____

6. All families respond to having a child with a disability in the same way._____

7. In the stage theory approach to describing parental reactions to the diagnosis of a disability the initial reaction is shock._____

8. Most couples who have a child with a disability ultimately divorce._____

Multiple Choice

1. A family systems model considers:
    a. family characteristics.
    b. family interactions.
    c. family functions.
    d. all of the above.

2. P. L. 94-142:
    a. requires family participation.
    b. considers families as less than full participants in the educational process.
    c. requires parents to participate in the developing of IEPs.
    d. none of the above.

3. Family functions include:
    a. affection
    b. self-esteem
    c. daily care
    d. none of the above

4. Cohesion refers to:
    a. degree of freedom and independence experienced by family members
    b. ability to change in response to a crisis
    c. recognition of positive contributions
    d. none of the above

5. A stage of the family life cycle includes:
   a. shock
   b. grief
   c. anger
   d. early childhood

6. The stage theory of parent reaction to disability includes:
   a. shock.
   b. socialization.
   c. mourning.
   d. none of the above.

7. The secondary phase of the stage theory of parental reaction includes:
   a. shock, denial, depression.
   b. ambivalence, guilt, anger.
   c. bargaining, adaptation, and acceptance.
   d. none of the above

8. Fathers of children with disabilities are:
   a. more accepting of their children than mothers.
   b. less emotional in their reaction to a diagnosis of disabilities.
   c. worried about day to day childcare.
   d. all of the above.

9. Grandparents of children with disabilities:
   a. go through various stages of acceptance.
   b. worry about their children and grandchildren.
   c. can serve as a source of emotional support.
   d. all of the above.

10. Families from various cultures:
    a. view disabilities differently.
    b. attribute their child's disability to the "Will of God".
    c. think of a disability as an overwhelming family shame.
    d. all of the above

Matching

1. family functions ___
2. primary phase ___
3. family life cycle ___
4. P. L. 94-142 ___
5. eugenics movement ___
6. anger ___
7. survivor's guilt ___
8. adaptability ___
9. Native American ___
10. family systems model ___

a. family's ability to change in response to stress
b. characteristics, interactions, functions, and life cycle of a family
c. part of the secondary phase of the stages of parental reaction to disabilities
d. first stage of parental reaction to a child with disabilities
e. have no word in language for disability
f. featured sterilization to reduce number of unfit parents
g. feelings due to absence of illness or disability in own life
h. affection, self-esteem, economics, daily care, education
i. requires that families participate in educational decisions affecting their children
j. early childhood, school age, adolescence, adulthood

Chapter 4: Parents, Families, And Exceptionality
Practice Test Answer Key

True or False
1. False. Professionals work with families of children with disabilities.
2. True
3. True
4. False. Parents are required to be part of the educational planning process as the result of the passage of P. L. 94-142.
5. True
6. False. Families pass through similar response stages to having a child with a disability. Responses, however, vary from one family to another.
7. True
8. False. Many researchers have found no difference in divorce rates between families with and without children with disabilities.

Multiple Choice
1. D
2. A and C
3. A, B, and C
4. A
5. D
6. A and C
7. B
8. B
9. D
10. D

Matching
1.   H
2.   D
3.   J
4.   I
5.   F
6.   C
7.   G
8.   A
9.   E
10. B

Check Your Understanding ⇨ **See textbook page 136**
Answer Key

1. How has the relationship between parents and professionals changed over the years? What circumstances have aided this process?

The relationship between parents and professionals has changed from adversarial and antagonistic to one of collaboration and cooperation. The passage of P. L. 94-142, with its amendments including IDEA, requires that parents participate in educational decisions concerning their children.

2. What was the purpose of the eugenics movement, and how did it affect relationships between professionals and parents?

The eugenics movement used sterilization to reduce the number of " unfit" parents and inferior offspring. The eugenics movement provided the basis for the belief that parents were the cause of their child's disability.

3. Why do professionals now believe that efforts should be directed toward working with families of children with special needs instead of just parents?

P. L. 99-457 and P. L. 101-476 changed the emphasis from working with parents to working with families. This resulted in a realization that collaboration should not only be with parents but should include other immediate and extended family members. Professionals now see families as coordinators and facilitators of service delivery.

4. Define the term collaboration as it pertains to professionals and parents.

Collaboration between professionals and parents means that professionals work collaboratively with families. Further, professionals do not have power over families but achieve power with families.

5. What is the rationale behind a family systems model?

The rationale behind the family systems model is that the family is an interrelated social system that operates as an interactive and interdependent unit.

6. Identify the four key components of Turnbull and Turnbull's family systems framework. Explain the characteristics of each of these elements.

The key components of Turnbull and Turnbull's family systems framework are family characteristics, family interaction, family functions, and family life cycle. Family characteristics include health statues, coping style, family size, socioeconomic status, and severity of disability. Family interactions include the degree of family cohesion and adaptability. Family functions include affection, self-esteem, economics, daily care, socializations, recreation, and education. Family life cycle is the developmental changes that occur in families over time. The life cycle usually includes the stages of early childhood, school age, adolescence, and adulthood.

7. How does the concept of cohesion differ from adaptability in the Turnbull model?

Cohesion is the degree of freedom and independence experienced by each member of the family. Adaptability is the family's ability to change in response to a crisis or stressful event. Both of these concepts occur along a continuum of freedom or rigidity.

8. What are the stages of emotional response that many parents go through when informed that their child has a disability? Give examples of the types of behavior typically exhibited at each stage.

The parents usually go through three stages over time in response to learning that they have a child with disabilities. The primary phase is characterized by shock, denial, grief, and depression. The secondary phase includes the reactions of ambivalence, guilt, anger, shame, and embarrassment. The tertiary phase includes the behavior of bargaining, adaptation and reorganization, and acceptance and adjustment. Parents often move back and forth in these stages over time.

9. What cautions does Garguilo stress when applying a stage theory model to parents of children with disabilities?

The stage theory approach has been criticized as being unduly negative, rigid, and lacking in empirical evidence. All families respond to news of a child with a disability in their own way. Finally, the order of family responses is not predictable and moving to the next phase does not indicate a complete resolution of feelings at the previous stage.

10. In what ways might a child with a disability affect his or her family?

The effect of a child with a disability on the family depends on parents' marital integration, religious beliefs and values, financial resources, cultural heritage, support systems, child's gender, and severity of the disability.

11. What does the research literature suggest about the impact of childhood disability on marital relationships, fathers, siblings, and grandparents of children with special needs?

The impact of a child with disabilities on marriage relationships is variable. Some research says divorce is higher in families with a disabled child while other research indicates that there is no difference. Research concerning fathers of children with disabilities indicates that fathers are less emotional in reaction, focus on long-term consequences, and influenced by visibility of the disability and the attitudes of other family members. Siblings of children with disabilities show varying reactions to the situation. The sibling's reaction can be positive or negative. The sibling's reaction is affected by parental attitude and expectation, family socioeconomic status, severity and type of impairment, family size, gender of the sibling, age spacing, child-rearing practices, cultural heritage, and availability of support systems. The presence of a child with a disability can lead to survivor's guilt, worry about catching the disability, and resentment concerning child-care responsibilities. It also can lead to more compassion, greater tolerance for others, and higher levels of empathy. The grandparents of children with disabilities are frequently worried about their own children and grandchildren. They can help by being alternate caregivers, doing daily errands, and providing emotional support.

12. Name five emotional responses typically exhibited by siblings of children with disabilities.

Emotional responses of siblings of children with disabilities include depression and social withdrawal, poor peer relationships, anger at excessive child-care requirements, survivor's guilt at absence of disability in their own lives, worries about catching the disability. Other reactions include greater tolerance toward others, increased compassion, and higher levels of empathy.

13. Why is an awareness of and sensitivity to cultural and linguistic differences important for professionals when working with families of children with disabilities?

A disability should be considered within a cultural context. Each culture defines what is deviant and what is normal. Families may see a disability as the result of violation of social taboos, intergenerational reprisals, "God's will" or overwhelming shame. Various perspectives about a disability can affect the interventions a family is willing to ask for and accept, degree of involvement in educational planning, and collaborative partnerships between families and professionals.

14. **Describe what you believe to be key personal characteristics of professionals who work with families of individuals with disabilities.**

Professionals who work with families of individuals with disabilities should show an awareness and sensitivity to the needs of families. They should facilitate interactions with families by genuinely caring. Professionals also need to have the characteristics of active listening, honesty, empathy, and genuineness in their work with children and their families.

CHAPTER FIVE
PERSONS WITH MENTAL RETARDATION

Overview of Persons with Mental Retardation

Chapter five is an overview of the field of mental retardation. The author emphasizes the different definitions and classification systems used in the area of mental retardation. Possible causes of mental retardation also are investigated. The chapter stresses the educational characteristics and possible classroom interventions to assist children with mental retardation. Finally, strategies are discussed to facilitate the transition of individuals with mental retardation into the employment arena.

Chapter Key Points

- Individuals with mental retardation have been classified using various conceptual models.
- Possible causes of mental retardation occur before birth, during birth, and after birth.
- Individuals with mental retardation often have problems attending to stimuli, a feeling of helplessness, and short-term memory.
- The need of a functional curriculum that stresses community based instruction is a key component of any curriculum for individuals with mental retardation.
- The principles of normalization, deinstitutionalization, and self-advocacy are essential for people with mental retardation.

Focus and Reflect

1. Discuss the support levels incorporated into the AAMR 1992 definition of mental retardation (limited, intermittent, extensive, and pervasive).

_____

_____

_____

2. Discuss three learning characteristics of individuals with mild mental retardation.

_____

_____

_____

3. Discuss the impact of poor prenatal care of the development of the unborn fetus.

_____

_____

_____

4. Discuss the transition needs of students entering the competitive employment workplace.

_____

_____

_____

Chapter Guided Review

1. Defining mental retardation
    a. 1961 definition-Intellectual functioning one standard deviation below the mean; adaptive behavior consideration first introduced
    b. 1973 definition –Intellectual functioning two standard deviations below the mean; adaptive behavior clarified
    c. 1983 definition- Similar to 1973 definition; more flexible on upper limits of MR to 70 – 75.
    d. 1992 definition- Mental retardation is a relationship between individual, environment, and support system.

2. Assessing intellectual ability
    a. Weschler Intelligence Scale for Children - III
    b. Stanford Benet Intelligence Scale - IV
    c. Cautions - Cultural bias, stability of IQ, overemphasis on IQ scores.

3. Adaptive Behavior
    a. AAMR Adaptive Behavior Scale- School
    b. AAMR Adaptive Behavior Scale- Residential and Community
    c. Vineland Adaptive Behavior Scales

4. Classifications of individuals with Mental retardation
    a. Etiological perspective
    b. Intellectual deficits- Mild, moderate, severe, profound.
    c. Educational perspective- Educable mentally retarded, trainable mentally retarded
    d. Levels of support- Intermittent, limited, extensive, and pervasive

5. History
    a. Greece and Rome- Cruel to infants with disabilities
    b. Middle Ages- Children with disabilities were "Children of God" or thought to be filled with Satan.
    c. Early optimism- Esqurial, Itard, Segiun, Howe: early pioneers in special education.
    d. Protector and pessimism- Sterilization; mental retardation equated with social problems; institutions deplorable and long term.
    e. Trends- Normalization; deinstitutionalization
    f. Emergence of public education for students who are mentally retarded- President's Committee on mental retardation; legislation to establish program for children.

6. Prevalence of Mental Retardation
    a. Downward shift in prevalence from 3 to 1% of the general population.
    b. Ninety percent in the mild category of mental retardation

7. Prenatal causes of Mental retardation
    a. Chromosomal abnormalities- Down syndrome; Fragile X syndrome
    b. Metabolic and nutritional disorders- Phenlketonuria (PKU); galactosemia
    c. Maternal infections- Rubella (German measles), syphilis, AIDS, Rh incompatibility, toxoplasmosis, and cytomegalovirus.

8. Perinatal Causes of Mental retardation
    a. Gestational disorders- Prematurity (birth prior to 37 weeks gestation); low birth weight (less than 5 pounds or 2500 grams); very low birth weight (less than 3 pounds or 1500 grams)
    b. Neonatal Complications- Anoxia, hypoxia, birth trauma, breech presentation, precipitous birth.

9. Postnatal causes of Mental retardation
    a.   Infections and Intoxicants- Lead poisoning, meningitis, encephalitis.
    b.   Environmental factors, Nutritional problems, inadequate health care, lack of early cognitive stimulation, adverse living conditions.

10. Prevention Strategies in Mental retardation
    a.   primary prevention- Eliminate problems before onset.
    b.   secondary prevention- Eliminate potential risk factors.
    c.   tertiary prevention- Seeks to minimize adverse consequences
    d.   Screening- Amniocentesis, chronic villus sampling, ultrasound.

11. Learning characteristics of Persons with Mental retardation
    a.   Attention- Difficulty in selective attention to relevant stimuli.
    b.   Memory- Inefficient rehearsal strategies; inability to generalize to novel situation.
    c.   Academic performances- Reading frequently weakest area.
    d.   Motivation- External focus of control, outer- directed, learned helplessness
    e.   Generalization- Difficulty duplicating learning with different cues, people, and environments
    f.   Language development- Higher IQ usually fewer language problems

12. Social and Behavioral Characteristics
    a.   Poor interpersonal skills
    b.   Socially inappropriate or immature behavior.

13. Education Considerations
    a.   51.6 percent of children with mental retardation are educated in a self-contained environment.
    b.   Functional curriculum- Life skills required for successful daily living; survival words, community based math concepts.
    c.   Community based instruction- instruction in natural settings
    d.   INCLUDE- Identify environmental demands, note student learning strengths and needs, check for areas of student success, look for problem areas, use information to develop adaptations, decide which adaptations to implement, evaluate student progress.
    e.   Task analysis- Complex behavior is broken down into sequenced into component points.
    f.   Cooperative learning- Small heterogeneous groups of learners involved in jointly accomplishing an activity.
    g.   Unit approach – Integration of language arts, reading, math, and daily living skill content areas.
    h.   Scaffolding- Support provided in the initial learning stages and then gradually removed to become more independent.

14. Services for young children with Mental retardation
    a.   Infant stimulation- Early stimulation for infants with severe developmental disabilities
    b.   At risk services- Environmentally at risk, biologically at risk.
    c.   Family-centered intervention - Stresses enabling and empowering families.
    d.   Best practice based: Comprehensive, normalized, outcome based, interaction between disabled and non-disabled children.

15. Transition to Adulthood
    a.   Individual transition plan - Starts at age 14; must be in place by age 16.
    b.   Sheltered workshops - Job training in a segregated environment; jobs low skill level and repetitive.
    c.   Supported employment - Job coach provides on the job assistance and support for the person with mental retardation; goal of competitive employment.

16. Adults with Mental retardation
    a. Normalization- Self-determination; self-advocacy
    b. Family issues- Worry about financial obligations, education concerns, impact of disability on siblings, long term care requirements.

17. Issues of diversity
    a. Overrepresentation of children of color in special education.
    b. Misdiagnosis, a reflection of cultural differences.

18. Technology and Persons with Mental retardation
    a. Assistive technology- Technology designed to assist people with disabilities.
    b. Technology expands access to general education curriculum.

19. Trends, Issues, Controversies
    a. More community based activities.
    b. Application of assistive technology to meet various needs of people with mental retardation.
    c. Emphases on quality of life and normalization.
    d. Growing geriatric population with Mental retardation.
    e. Interventions will result in smaller number of people being identified as mentally retarded.
    f. More inclusive educational placements for students with mental retardation.
    g. Greater attention to self-advocacy and self-determination for individuals with mental retardation.

Application Exercises & Project Suggestions
1. Read the book *Christmas in Purgatory* by Burton Blatt. List seven changes that have been made in services provided by institutions to individuals with mental retardation since the publication of the book in the 1960s.
2. Interview a family of a child with Down syndrome. Ask what are the challenges and rewards the family has experienced because of this child as a family member.
3. Observe a classroom serving children with severe profound mental retardation. List four ways that the curriculum in this classroom differs from program objectives for children with mild mental retardation.

InfoTrac® Article Suggestions

Activity 5.1: Folic acid
This activity is based on an article that investigates the impact of folic acid on the developing fetus.
1. Locate and read **"Lack of Folic Acid Continues to Causes Preventable Birth Defects"**.

2. What two conditions can be reduced or prevented by extra folic acid in the diet of the mother.

_____

_____

_____

3. What daily level of folic acid is recommended for pregnant women?

_____

_____

_____

4. List three interventions, which might assist individuals in obtaining appropriate levels of folic acid.

_____

_____

_____

Activity 5.2: Down syndrome
This activity explores the effect of family life on the intellectual growth of children with disabilities.

1. Locate and read **"Disabilities Develop as Family Affair"** by B. Bower found in *Science News.*

2. Discuss the role of the child's motivation on intellectual development.

_____

_____

_____

3. Discuss the impact of a warm response mother on acquiring problems solving and daily living skills.

_____

_____

_____

4. Why do you think parents of children with disabilities experience stress, isolation, and depression related to child-rearing as their children approach adolescence?

_____

_____

_____

InfoTrac® Article Suggestions

- Honein, M., Paulozzi, L., & Mathews, T. (2001). Impact of folic acid fortification on incidence of neural tube defects, Science News, 20, 15.
- Cuckle, H. (2001). Time for total shift to first-trimester screening for Down syndrome. The Lancet, 358, 1658.

Key Terms

Define each:

standard deviation _____

adaptive behavior_____

educable mentally retarded_____

trainable mentally retarded_____

level of support_____

natural supports_____

formal supports_____

normalization_____

deinstitutionalization_____

etiology_____

prenatal_____

perinatal_____

postnatal_____

Down syndrome_____

Fragile X syndrome_____

phenylketonuria (PKU)_____

glactosemia_____

rubella_____

syphilis_____

AIDS_____

Rh incompatibility_____

Toxoplasmosis_____

cytomegalovirus_____

fetal alcohol syndrome_____

fetal alcohol effect_____

anencephaly_____

microcephaly_____

hydrocephalus_____

low birth weight_____

premature birth_____

anoxia_____

hypoxia_____

birth trauma_____

breech presentation_____

precipitous birth_____

lead poisoning_____

meningitis_____

encephalitis_____

primary prevention_____

secondary prevention_____

tertiary prevention_____

amniocentesis_____

chorionic villus sampling_____

ultrasound_____

therapeutic abortion_____

spina bifida_____

external locus of control_____

learned helplessness_____

outer-directedness_____

generalizing _____

functional curriculum_____

functional academics_____

community-based instruction_____

task analysis_____

cooperative learning_____

unit method_____

scaffolding_____

infant stimulation_____

environmentally at risk_____

established risk_____

biologically at-risk_____

family-centered early intervention_____

sheltered workshop_____

supported competitive employment_____

job coach_____

self-determination_____

self-advocacy_____

instructional technology_____

assistive technology_____

CHAPTER FIVE: PERSONS WITH MENTAL RETARDATION
Practice Test

True or False

1. A widely used assessment of intelligence is the Wechsler Intelligence Scale for Children. _____

2. The 1992 definition of mental retardation stressed classifications based on intellectual performance. _____

3. IQ remains stable throughout a person's lifetime. _____

4. Adaptive behavior is the degree to which an individual meets the standards of maturation, learning, personal independence, and social responsibility expected for his/her age or cultural group. _____

5. The classifications of mild, moderate, severe, and profound mental retardation focus on intellectual functioning. _____

6. In early Greece and Rome, children with disabilities were considered "Children of God". _____

7. In the Middle Ages it was not uncommon for individuals with mental retardation to be sent to prison and kept in chains. _____

8. Down syndrome is caused by a viral infection. _____

Multiple Choice

1. The current estimated prevalence of mental retardation in the general population is:
   a. 3 %
   b. 1%
   c. 20%
   d. 15%

2. Itard was considered the "Father of Special Education" because of his work with:
   a. Howe
   b. Seguin
   c. Victor
   d. Dix

3. Down syndrome children:
   a. may have a greater risk of developing Alzheimer's disease.
   b. frequently have trisomy 21
   c. often function at the moderate level of mental retardation
   d. all of the above

4. Phenylketonuria is caused by:
   a. an inability to process phenylalanine
   b. requires a strict diet to control impact
   c. is caused by an extra chromosome
   d. both A and B

5. Fetal alcohol syndrome:
   a. is controlled by drinking a safe level during pregnancy
   b. is caused by drinking during pregnancy
   c. is totally preventable by not drinking at all
   d. both B and C

6. The effects of Rh incompatibility are controlled by:
   a. limiting a family to one child
   b. use of rhogam shot within 72 hours of birth or the termination of a pregnancy
   c. use of a strict diet
   d. all of the above

7. Low birth weight is considered:
   a. 8 pounds or less at birth
   b. 3 pounds, 5 ounces or less at birth
   c. 5 pounds, 8 ounces or less at birth
   d. none of the above

8. Neonatal complications at birth include:
   a. anoxia
   b. hypoxia
   c. breech presentation
   d. all of the above

9. Meningitis is a viral infection affecting:
   a. the brain
   b. the brain and spinal cord covering tissue (meninges)
   c. the heart
   d. the kidneys

10. Environmental factors that may cause mental retardation are:
   a. child abuse
   b. neglect
   c. nutritional problems
   d. lack of early cognitive stimulation
   e. all of the above

Matching

1. Rhogam shot ___
2. Anoxia ___
3. Seguin ___
4. Howe ___
5. external locus of control ___
6. cytomegalovirus ___
7. amniocentesis
8. hydrocephalus ___
9. task analysis ___
10. functional academics ___

a. outcomes of behavior are events beyond one's control
b. lack of oxygen
c. blockage of cerebrospinal fluid resulting in enlarged cranial cavity
d. test to detect deformities in the developing fetus
e. first president of AAMR and wrote first method book in mental retardation
f. common virus that is part of the herpes group which can cause defects in the developing fetus
g. given within 72 hours of birth
h. complex task is broken down and sequenced into its component parts
i. a curriculum focusing on independent living skills, community resources, and personal hygiene
j. established a residential program for individuals with mental retardation at the Perkins Institute for the Blind

Chapter 5: Persons with Mental Retardation
Practice Test Answer Key

True or False
1. True
2. False. The 1992 definition of mental retardation stressed the interaction between the individual, the environment, and needed supports.
3. False. Intelligence is not static but capable of changing.
4. True
5. True
6. False. In early Greece and Rome, children with disabilities were often thrown off of cliffs or placed in large earthen jars.
7. True
8. False. Down syndrome is caused by non-disjunction at conception and is related to the age of the parents.

Multiple Choice
1. B
2. C
3. D
4. D
5. D
6. B
7. C
8. D
9. B
10. E

Matching
1. G
2. B
3. E
4. J
5. A
6. F
7. D
8. C
9. H
10. I

Check Your Understanding ⇨ See textbook page 193
Answer Key

1. How has the definition of mental retardation changed over the past 3 decades?
In 1961 mental retardation was considered one standard deviation from the mean (IQ of 85 or 4) and the concept of adaptive behavior was introduced. In 1973 mental retardation was redefined as two standard deviations below the mean and more attention was given to adaptive behavior. The 1983 definition was much like the 1973 definition. It extended the IQ score up to 75 for individuals with mental retardation. The 1997 definition looked at mental retardation as a relationship between the individual, the environment, and the type of support required for maximum functioning in various settings.

2. Identify the 3 key elements of the 1992 AAMR definition of mental retardation. How are they conceptually interrelated?
The three elements are the individual, the environment, and the level of support. The person's capabilities within various environments are seen as a reflection of supports received to function at the highest level of independence.

3. Why is assessment of intelligence such a controversial issue?
Often there is a potential for cultural bias in tests, IQ scores are capable of changing, and IQ scores are not the sole indication of a person's ability.

4. What is adaptive behavior and how is it assessed?
Adaptive behavior is the degree to which a person meets the standards of maturation, learning, personal independence, and social responsibility that are expected by his/her age level and cultural group. Frequently, the most used assessment instruments in adaptive behavior are the AAMR Adaptive Behavior Scale-School, AAMR Adaptive Behavior Scale-Residential and Community, and the Vineland Adaptive Behavior Scales.

5. List four different strategies for classifying individuals with mental retardation.
Four strategies used in classifying individuals with mental retardation include etiology, intellectual functioning (mild, moderate, severe, and profound), education perspective (educable mentally retarded, trainable mentally retarded), level of support (intermittent, limited, extensive, and pervasive).

6. How has society's view and understanding of person s with mental retardation changed over the centuries?
In Greece and Rome, children with disabilities were either killed or left in jars. In the Middle Ages, in Europe, people with disabilities were viewed as "Children of God", natural fools, or filled with Satan. In the early 1800s, Esquirol, Seguin, Itard, and Howe started treatment programs for the disabled. In the early 1900s sterilization and warehousing of individuals with mental retardation in institutions were initiated. In the 1960s and 1970s, trends in mental retardation included research, education, normalization, and deinstitutionalization.

7. What factors have contributed to the gradual reduction in the number of individuals classified as mentally retarded?
Factors which have lead to a lower number of individuals being classified as mentally retarded include prevention and early intervention efforts, changes in the definition of mental retardation, the impact of litigation, changes in referral practices, placement of higher functioning students with mental retardation in programs for learning disabilities, and reluctance to identify children as mildly mentally retarded.

8. **Mental retardation is often the result of various etiological factors. List seven possible causes of mental retardation and give an example of each.**
Possible causes of mental retardation include chromosomal abnormalities (Down syndrome), metabolic and nutritional disorders (phenylketonuria-PKU), maternal infections (rubella), environmental causes (fetal alcohol syndrome), cranial malformation (hydrocephalus), gestational disorders (premature birth), and neonatal complications (anoxia).

9. **How do learned helplessness, outer-directedness, and generalizing affect learning in students with mental retardation?**
Outer-directedness is a loss of confidence in one's own abilities and a reliance on others for cues. Learned helplessness is an expectancy of failure, which causes students with mental retardation to stop trying. Generalizing is using a mastered skill in new or different settings. Individuals with mental retardation have difficulty duplicating the skill when confronted with different cues, different people, or different environments.

10. **Define the term functional academics. How are functional academics related to the concept of community-based instruction?**
Functional academics instruct students in life skills and prepare them for living environments after leaving school. Functional academics focus on personal hygiene, independent living skills, and community resources. A functional curriculum is often taught in community-based instruction. This eliminates any generalization of skills from one setting to another.

11. **What is cooperative learning, and why is it a popular instructional technique?**
Cooperative learning encourages children of varying skills to work together to achieve a common goal. Cooperative learning is growing in popularity because it emphasizes cooperation rather than competition among students.

12. **List and describe the necessary steps for effectively using scaffolding with students with mental retardation.**
Scaffolding introduces the concept, regulates the difficulty of tasks during guided practice, provides various contexts for practice, provides feedback to the student, increases student responsibility for learning, and provides independent practice of the skill.

13. **How has family centered early intervention influenced programming activities for young children with mental retardation?**
The curriculum in early childhood intervention is based on the individual needs of the child and his/her family. The early childhood curriculum seeks to enable and empower families. These programs are comprehensive, for children and families.

14. **Distinguish between a sheltered workshop for adults with mental retardation and the contemporary practice of supported employment.**
Sheltered workshops are large facilities that provide job training in a segregated environment. The jobs are of short duration and offer minimal job training. Supported employment emphasizes training in a competitive work environment. Individuals with mental retardation who are trained using the supported employment model tend to function better in competitive employment than those who have been trained in sheltered workshops.

15. **What is assistive technology, and how might it benefit individuals who are mentally retarded?**
Assistive technology is specifically designed to assist people with disabilities. Technology can expand access to the general education curriculum for individuals with mental retardation. Specific applications are drill and practice, games, simulations, and writing and reading content area assistance.

CHAPTER SIX
PERSONS WITH LEARNING DISABILITIES

Overview of Persons with Learning Disabilities

Chapter Six presents an overview of the field of learning disabilities. Various definitions of learning disabilities. Also a history of the various stages of development of learning disabilities is presented. The chapter also investigates possible causes of learning disabilities. Assessment and intervention alternatives also are presented. Finally, the chapter looks at the needs of individuals with learning disabilities through the life span.

Chapter Key Points

- There are various definitions of learning disabilities.
- Although the cause of learning disabilities is not known, causal research is being conducted in the areas of central nervous system damage, heredity, biochemical abnormalities, and environmental factors.
- The field of learning disabilities has evolved throughout the late nineteenth and twentieth century.
- Learning disabilities is the fastest growing and now the largest population serviced by special education services.
- A variety of assessments and curricular interventions are suggested to assist children and adults with learning disabilities.
- Technology is critical in helping children with learning disabilities in a variety of academic areas.
- Transition plans assist individuals with disabilities in planning for post-secondary services.

Focus and Reflect

Discuss the model of learning strategies used with children with learning disabilities

_____

_____

_____

Discuss portfolios as a means of informal assessment for children with learning disabilities

_____

_____

_____

Discuss the concept of discrepancy between achievement and potential in the identification of children with learning disabilities

_____

_____

_____

List the emphasis of the foundation, transition, integration, and current phases in the development of the field of learning disabilities

_____

_____

Chapter Guided Review

1. Learning disabilities definition
   a. most frequent definition used is from P.L. 94-142
   b. many definitions of learning disabilities from various groups
   c. common components of definitions of disabilities are intelligence within normal range, discrepancy between potential and actual achievement, not caused by other disabilities, difficulty in one or more academic areas, and presumption of CNS dysfunction.
2. History of learning disabilities
   a. foundation phase- focus on traumatic brain injuries; key persons: Hinshelwood, Strauss, and Goldstein
   b. transition phase- development of assessment instruments and remediation strategies in learning disabilities; key persons: Orton, Fernald, Kephart, Frostig
   c. integration phase- term learning disabilities coined, school based programs initiated, establishment of advocacy organization in learning disabilities; key persons: Kirk, Minskoff, Hammill, Larsen, and Wilderholt
   d. current phase- issues: inclusion, diverse learners, technology, assessment, and ADHD; key persons: Mercer, Learner, Hallahan, Kauffman, and others
3. Prevalence of learning disabilities
   a. learning disabilities have grown 25% over the last 22 years
   b. 5.7% of students population ages 6-17
   c. greater increase caused by greater public awareness, improved assessment procedures, and high social acceptance of label.
4. Etiology of learning disabilities
   a. acquired trauma- prenatal causes (smoking, drugs, and use of alcohol),perinatal causes (prolonged delivery, anoxia, prematurity, forceps), and postnatal causes (strokes, concussions, high fever, head injury, meningitis/encephalitis).
   b. genetic/hereditary influences- some types of learning disabilities are inherited
   c. biochemical abnormalities- Feingold/allergic reaction theory; megavitamin theory
   d. environmental possibilities- low social economic status, malnutrition, lack of access to health care, quality of instruction from teachers.
5. Characteristics of Persons with Learning Disabilities
   a. disorders of attention- attention deficit disorders/attention deficit hyperactivity disorder, 20-40% ADHD in children with learning disabilities
   b. poor motor abilities
   c. psychological process deficits
   d. lack of cognitive strategies needed for efficient learning
   e. oral language difficulties- functional use of language problems in syntax, semantics, phonology
   f. reading difficulties- primary reason for school failure; dyslexia
   g. written language problems- spelling, handwriting, composition problems
   h. quantitative disorders- computational skills, word problems, spatial relationships, writing numbers, and coping shapes
   i. social skills deficits- low self-esteem, low self-concept, inept of intercepting social cues
   j. boys identified four times more than girls
   k. interaction of social/emotional problems, academic difficulties, and cognitive deficits
   l. memory- problems in short-term and working memory
   m. metacognition- problems in recognition of task requirement, implementation of appropriate process, and adjusting one's own performance to ensure successful task completion.
   n. Attributions- learned helplessness, inactive/inefficient learners
7. Assessment of Learning Disabilities

    a. assessment decisions- Wechsler Intelligence Scale for children-III, Stanford-Binet Intelligence Scale (4th edition), achievement tests (Wechsler Individual Achievement Test)

    b. assessment strategies- norm-referenced assessments, criteria- referenced assessments

    c. curriculum- based assessment test items based on classroom curriculum

    d. Portfolio assessment- collection of student work overtime, children's journals, quizzes, worksheets, projects, and reports

8. Educated Considerations

    a. educational placements of children with learning disabilities- 44% regular classroom, 39% resource room

    b. instructional approaches, one placement inclusion does not fit the needs of all children with learning disabilities; educational approaches should be validated

    c. cognitive training- self-instruction of children verbalizing instructions to themselves; mnemonic strategies used to recall facts on relationships

    d. direct instruction- explicit step by step strategy, using task analysis development of mastery at each step, process of correction of student error, fading of teacher-directed activities, systematic practice, review of newly learned concepts

    e. learning strategies- Strategic Instruction Model: pretest learner, describe learning strategy, model strategy, student verbally practices strategy, controlled feedback, practice on authentic task, post-test learner, generalization

9. Intervention for Students with Attention Deficit Hyperactivity Disorder

    a. functional assessment- identify antecedents and consequences of behavior

    b. self-regulation- self-control strategy that includes self-observation, self-assessment, self-recording, self-determination of reinforcement, and self-administration of reinforcement

    c. home-school collaboration- use of journals, checklists, traveling notebooks

    d. instructional modification- place in least distracting class location, surround with good role models, have low pupil-teacher ratio, avoid unnecessary changes in schedules, maintain eye contact, use multi-sensory teaching strategies, help student organize, break work into smaller segments, alternate seating, check homework assignment before leaving school, use learning aids, work with peers

    e. medication-Ritalin, Cylert, Dexedrine most commonly used

10. Service for Young Children with Learning Disabilities

    a. not labeled in preschool years

    b. states have until age nine to label children

    c. developmental model-cognitive development based on interaction with environment

    d. behavioral model-direct instruction and precise sequence of instructional activities

    e. functional curriculum-stress on acquisition of age appropriate skills

11. Transition to Adulthood

    a. 38% of children with learning disabilities graduate from high school

    b. transition plan-statement of transition needs by age 14; statement of interagency responsibilities

    c. plan includes vocational training, employment options, preparation for college, preparation for independent living

12. Adults with Learning Disabilities

    a. drive to take control of own lives essential for independent living

    b. 4% of adults with learning disabilities attend college

    c. modification for adults with learning disabilities include adjustments in course requirements and evaluations, modification of program requirements, and auxiliary aids

13. Family Issues

    a. most families well adjusted

    b. brother and sisters adjust well to sibling with learning disabilities

    c. parents- consumers, advocates, managers of behavior; need own lives

14. Issues of Diversity
    a. dramatic negative effect of poverty on achievement
    b. disproportionate number of cultural and racial minority students in special education
15. Technology and Students with Learning disabilities
    a. assistive technology to compensate for barriers in learning
    b. academic computer programs: writing, mathematical problem solving, spelling
16. Trends, Issues and Controversies
    a. challenges in service delivery – full inclusion movement; consideration needed for a cascade of services for children with learning disabilities
    b. educational reform movement – higher drop out rates for high school students with learning disabilities resulting from high academic standards and required participation in state and local academic assessments.

Application Exercises & Project Suggestions

1. Observe an inclusive classroom serving children with learning disabilities. Observe a resource program serving children with learning disabilities. Compare the content of assistance provided to children by the two programs

2. Interview an adult with learning disabilities. Report on four challenges or adaptations that the adult faces in his/her daily life.

3. Attend a meeting of an advocacy group (ex. Association for Citizens with Learning Disabilities) in the area of learning disabilities.

InfoTrac® Suggestions

Activity 6.1: Attention deficit/hyperactivity disorder
This article discusses attention deficit/hyperactivity disorder. It lists a number of characteristics of children with this disorder and suggests intervention strategies.

1. Locate and read the article **"ADHD and Your School-Aged Child: from the American Academy of Pediatrics' Parent Pages"** found in the ***Brown University Child and Adolescent Behavior Letter***.

2. Discuss two components of a long term management plan for children with attention deficit/hyperactivity disorder.

_____

_____

_____

3. What types of research are taking place concerning attention deficit/hyperactivity disorder?

_____

_____

_____

4. List three characteristics of children with attention deficit/hyperactivity disorder.

_____

_____

Activity 6.2: Learning Disabilities
This article considers various definitions of children with learning disabilities. In addition, it evaluates the use of various psychological tests in the identification of children with learning disabilities.

1. Locate and read the article **"Learning Disabilities, Schooling, and Society"** by Robert Sternberg in ***Phi Delta Kappan***.

2. Discuss the concept that learning disabilities is a function of the demands of society.

_____

_____

_____

3. Discuss the concept that curriculum should value a wide range of learning and thinking abilities.

_____

_____

_____

4. Discuss the idea that children should be identified for service by levels of achievement rather than discrepancy between potential and achievement.

_____

_____

_____

InfoTrac® Article Suggestions
- Sternberg, R., & Grigorenko, E. (2001). Learning disabilities, schooling, and society. Phi Delta Kappan, 83, 335-341.
- Bower, B. (2001). Math fears subtract from memory, learning. Science News, 159, 405.

Key Terms
Define each:

learning disabilities_____

discrepancy_____

exclusionary clause_____

brain injury_____

familiarity studies_____

heritability studies_____

dyslexia_____

phonological awareness_____

pragmatics_____

short-term memory_____

working memory_____

metacognition_____

learned helplessness_____

attention deficit hyperactivity disorder (ADHD)_____

norm-referenced assessments_____

criterion-referenced assessment_____

curriculum-based assessment_____

authentic assessment_____

self-instruction_____

mnemonic strategies_____

direct instruction (DI)_____

task analysis_____

learning strategies_____

multimodal interventions_____

functional assessment_____

self-regulation_____

developmental/cognitive model_____

behavioral curriculum model_____

functional curriculum_____

transition plan_____

assistive technology_____

CHAPTER SIX: PERSONS WITH LEARNING DISABILITIES
Practice Test

True or False
1. The term learning disabilities is easily defined._____

2. Samuel Kirk coined the term learning disabilities._____

3. The foundation phase in learning disabilities focused on individuals with brain damage._____

4. Fernald believed that learning disabilities were a consequence of visual perceptual

   problems._____

5. The bulk of children with learning disabilities receiving services are between the ages of ten

   and thirteen._____

6. In a majority of cases, there is definitive evidence of brain damage as a cause of learning

   disabilities._____

7. Some types of learning disabilities are inherited._____

8. At times, learning disabilities are caused by poor teaching._____

Multiple Choice
1. Some of the characteristics of children with learning disabilities include
   a. hyperactivity.
   b. disorders of attention.
   c. language deficits.
   d. all of the above.

2. Boys are:
   a. four times more likely as girls to be identified as learning disabled.
   b. two times more likely as girls to be identified as learning disabled.
   c. not likely to be identified as learning disabled.
   d. none of the above

3. Dyslexia refers to:
   a. reading problems
   b. math problems
   c. writing problems
   d. speaking problems

4. Math problems experienced by children with learning disabilities include:
   a. computational problems
   b. word problems
   c. problems writing numbers
   d. all of the above

5. Poor penmanship results from:
   a. being left handed
   b. being right handed
   c. absence of needed fine motor skills
   d. lack of understanding of spatial relationships

6. The functional use of language in social situations is called:
    a. syntax
    b. phonology
    c. pragmatics
    d. semantics

7. Metacognition is:
    a. another name for learned helplessness.
    b. the ability to evaluate and monitor one's own performance.
    c. short term memory.
    d. none of the above.

8. Some facts concerning children with attention deficit hyperactivity disorder include the following statements:
    a. most outgrow it.
    b. diagnosed easily.
    c. persistent pattern of inattention and/or impulsivity.
    d. involves parents, teachers, and professionals in assessment activities.

9. Criterion referenced tests are:
    a. frequently given in the classroom.
    b. measure a student's performance against a predetermined criterion.
    c. are often used in developing educational objectives.
    d. all of the above.

10. Most students with learning disabilities receive services in
    a. resource programs.
    b. self-contained classes.
    c. a regular classroom inclusive environment.
    d. in separate schools.

Matching

1. Portfolio assessment ___
2. normed referenced tests ___
3. criterion referenced tests ___
4. Kirk ___
5. Fernald ___
6. direct instruction ___
7. learning strategies ___
8. functional assessment ___
9. Ritalin ___
10. transition plan ___

a. stressed multi-sensory approach (VAKT) in helping children

b. a plan to assist students with disabilities in planning for post-secondary services

c. determining the purpose or function of a behavior

d. measure student's performance against a predetermined criterion or mastery level

e. collection of samples of a student's work gathered over a period of time

f. focuses on components of the task or concept to be learned

g. focuses on how students learn and how to become a more purposeful and efficient learner

h. coined the term learning disabilities

i. individual performance is compared to a normative group

j. a medication frequently used with children with attention deficit hyperactivity disorders.

Chapter 5: Learning Disabilities
Practice Test Answer Key

True or False
1. False- Learning disabilities are not easily defined because of the many professionals involved in the field and the great number of learning problems included under the umbrella of this term.
2. True
3. True
4. False- Fernald advocated a multisensory approach to helping children with learning disabilities.
5. True
6. False- In a majority of cases, there is no definitive evidence of brain damage as a cause of learning disabilities.
7. True
8. True

Multiple Choice
1. D
2. A
3. A
4. D
5. C and D
6. C
7. B
8. C and D
9. D
10. C

Matching
1. E
2. I
3. D
4. H
5. A
6. F
7. G
8. C
9. J
10. B

1. Developing a definition of learning disabilities has proven to be problematic. Describe three reasons why this process has been so challenging.

Different disciplines serve children with learning disabilities. Also various terms have been consolidated into what is now learning disabilities. Finally learning disabilities is an umbrella concept that includes many types of learning problems.

2. What are the main components of most definitions of learning disabilities?

The common components of the learning disabilities definition are normal intellectual functioning, discrepancy between assumed and actual achievement, learning disabilities not caused by other disabilities, difficulty in one or more academic areas, and presumed central nervous system dysfunction.

3. Identify the four historical phases and their respective contributions to the development of the field of learning disabilities.

The foundation phase emphasized research with individuals who had suffered brain damage. The transition phase emphasized assessment and educational remediation strategies. The integration phase stresses school based programs, development of advocacy organizations in learning disabilities, and coining the term learning disabilities. The current phase focuses on the controversial issue of high academic standards and full inclusion as they impact individuals with learning disabilities.

4. List four possible causes of learning disabilities. Give an example of each.

Possible causes of learning disabilities include acquired trauma (ex. prenatal use of alcohol by mother), genetic/heredity influences (ex. inherited learning disabilities), biochemical abnormalities (ex. allegoric reactions to artificial colorings, flavorings, and additives), and environmental causes (ex. malnutrition and poor teaching).

5. Identify and describe five learning and behavioral characteristics common to individuals with learning disabilities. In your opinion, which of these deficits is the most debilitating. Why?

Five characteristics of children with learning disabilities are hyperactivity, disorders of attention, oral language difficulties, reading difficulties, and written language problems. Reading difficulties seem to be the most debilitating because this disability seems to permeate all academic areas including reading, math, oral language, and written language.

6. Do you think attention deficit hyperactivity disorder (ADHD) should be recognized as a disability category according to IDEA? Support your position.

(Responses will vary.)

7. Distinguish between norm-referenced and criterion-referenced assessments. What type of information does each test provide?

Norm-referenced assessments compare an individual's performance to a normative group of peers. This provides information for identification purposes but is weak in providing instructional direction. Criterion-referenced tests measure students' abilities against a predetermined criterion or mastery level. These tests help to determine if a child has mastered specific skill. It is also helpful in instructional planning, monitoring progress, towards meeting educational goals, and making decisions about children.

8. **What is the current trend in educational placement of students with learning disabilities? Do you agree with this trend? Why?**

The current trend in educational placement of children with learning disabilities is a shift away from resource room placement. This reflects a trend towards inclusive placements of children with disabilities.

9. **Identify the major components of the following instructional approaches used with children who are learning disables: cognitive training, direct instruction, and learning strategies. What are the advantages and disadvantages of each approach?**

Cognitive training attempts to modify a student's underlying thought patterns to affect observable changes in performance. Cognitive training is helpful in remediating many academic difficulties. Direct instruction consists of an explicit step-by-step strategy, having mastery at each step. Correct student errors, gradual fading of teacher direction, systematic practice, and cumulative review of newly learned concepts. Direct instruction results in significant gains in academic learning. Learning strategies teaches children how to learn and how to become purposeful and efficient learners. The Strategic Instruction Model stresses obtaining a commitment from the pupil, describing the learning strategy, student verbally practices strategy, learner engages in practice and feedback, student practices on authentic tasks, post-test, generalization. This model helps students with learning disabilities to function in a regular classroom.

10. **What role does medication play in the treatment of attention deficit hyperactivity disorder (ADHD)? Why is the strategy controversial? Describe three other intervention options for students with ADHD.**

Medication allows students to concentrate better, increase attention span, and control impulsivity and distractibility. Medication is ineffective in 25-30% of individuals. In addition, medication has side effects of irritability, insomnia, growth retardation, weight loss, depression, loss of appetite, headaches, and nausea. Other intervention strategies for children with ADHD include self-regulation, home-school collaboration, and instructional modification. Self-regulation requires students to stop and compare their behavior to a criterion. They are rewarded if the behavior matches the criterion. Home-school relationships are critical in monitoring medication effects, completing homework, and developing behavior plans. Instruction modifications include placing children in the least distracting place in the class, surrounding the student with good role models, maintaining low-pupil-teacher ratio, providing multi-sensory cues, and maintaining eye contact with children.

11. **Why is it difficult to determine if a preschooler is learning disabled?**

Often preschoolers are at risk for disabilities. As a result of early intervention they may never be classified as disabled. Also most placement criteria stress a discrepancy between academic potential and achievement. Such a discrepancy does not exist at the preschool level.

12. **What unique problems confront secondary students with learning problems? How can public schools help adolescents meet these challenges?**

Secondary students have a history of failure at academic tasks, diminished self-concept, lack of motivation, and a degree of social ineptness. Public schools can help these students through the development of transition plans that address postsecondary training, independent living, and future employment

13. **Describe the variables that contribute to the successful adjustment of adults with learning disabilities.**

Variables which lead to success are a desire to take control of one's life, perseverance, acknowledging limitations, coping strategies, support systems, motivation, creative ways to compensate, emotional stability, and a positive attitude.

14. **In what ways might an individual with learning disabilities affect his or her family?**

Parents experience stress in coping with their child's learning disability. Siblings often experience feeling of embarrassment, anger, and resentment concerning the child with learning disabilities.

15. Why is it difficult to distinguish between cultural/linguistic differences and a learning disability?

It is difficult to distinguish between learning problems resulting from cultural differences and learning problems resulting from learning disabilities. Teachers have to distinguish between cultural and linguistic differences and disabilities.

16. How can technology be used to benefit individuals with learning disabilities?

Students with learning disabilities use technology to compensate for barriers in learning. Helpful technology includes the Internet, word processing videodiscs, CD-ROMs, and interactive computer programs in various academic areas.

17. Describe two contemporary issues confronting the field of learning disabilities. How will these challenges affect programs for children and adolescents with learning disabilities?

Two issues facing the field of learning disabilities are the full inclusion movement and the educational reform movement. The full inclusion movement actually may have a negative impact on students. Educators need to consider a full spectrum of placement options to best meet the needs of students with learning disabilities. The educational reform movement seeks to raise academic standards. Students with learning disabilities will have great difficulty in meeting the higher levels of academic standards. Also students with learning disabilities have to be part of state and district testing. Often the tests are beyond the skill levels of this population of students.

CHAPTER SEVEN
PERSONS WITH EMOTIONAL OR BEHAVIORAL DISORDERS

Overview of Persons with Emotional or Behavioral Disorders

In this chapter the author examines many of the controversies that surround the identification and education of students with emotional or behavioral disorders. Characteristics, assessments, and educational interventions are discussed along with transitional planning methods.

Chapter Key Points

- The lack of a universally accepted definition of emotional and behavioral disorders causes professionals to struggle with issues of definition, classification and terminology.
- The federal definition of emotional and behavioral disorders excludes students considered socially maladjusted.
- A new definition of emotional and behavioral disorders was formulated in 1990.
- Students within the category of emotional or behavioral disorders are considered to be the most under-identified category of special education.
- Early identification holds the answer to decreasing the number of students with emotional and behavioral disorders.
- Interventions have shifted from reactive to proactive efforts.
- Collaborative efforts emphasizing the family in designing integrated services promise more positive outcomes for students with emotional or behavioral disorders.

Focus and Reflect

1. Discuss the implications of using the behavioral conceptual model on students with emotional or behavioral disorders.

_____

_____

_____

2. Discuss behaviors that may indicate a person is suicidal.

_____

_____

_____

3. List behaviors that students with emotional or behavioral disorders exhibit which make them unsuccessful in retaining friendships.

_____

_____

_____

Chapter Guided Review

1. The education and proper placement of students with emotional or behavioral disorders has been a source of controversy.

2. Due to issues related to definition, classification and terminology, there is widespread disagreement between professionals concerning the category of behavioral or emotional disorders.

3. The federal definition of emotional or behavioral disorders excludes individuals considered to be socially maladjusted.

4. In 1990 the Mental Health and Special Education Coalition proposed a new definition that seems to add a larger scope to emotional and behavioral disorders than the federal definition.

5. In an effort to improve identification two classification systems have been devised:
   a. clinically derived classification group behaviors into diagnostic categories which have criteria for diagnosis
   b. statistically derived classification uses the student's behavior patterns as the basis for diagnosis

6. Historically, the field of emotional and behavioral disorders has been tied to the fields of mental retardation, psychiatry and psychology.
   a. Lauretta Bender opened the Bellevue School in Bellevue Psychiatric Clinic in 1934.
   b. In 1940-1960 many experimental programs for emotional or behavioral disordered youth were established.
   c. In the 1960's conceptual models appeared in professional literature.
   d. In 1975, PL 94-142 included emotional or behavioral disorders as a category.

7. Less than one percent of the school-age population receives special education services for emotional or behavioral disorders although prevalence estimates are much higher.

8. Biological factors affect the development of emotional and behavioral disorders.
   a. lead poisoning
   b. injury
   c. poor nutrition
   d. infection
   e. exposure to toxins
   f. infant temperament

9. Environmental factors produce risk factors for conduct disorders.
   a. parental discord
   b. parental mental illness
   c. large family size and overcrowding in the home
   d. neglect and abuse
   e. poverty

10. Students with emotional or behavioral disorders display a variety of characteristics.
    a. low-average intelligence
    b. difficulty making and maintaining friendships
    c. difficulties in the social use of language

11. Assessment strategies for students with emotional or behavioral disorders must include a variety of sources of information and use a variety of methods due to the many facets of behavior and the variability in cultural and societal norms of behavior.

12. Intervention strategies for students include changing the environment, academic and instructional accommodations and behavioral modifications.
    a. physical environment changes include time management, transition management and classroom arrangement
    b. academic and instructional interventions include mnemonic strategies, self-monitoring strategies, curriculum –based measurements, and content enhancements
    c. behavioral modifications include establishment of classroom rules and promoting student's self-regulating behaviors

13. Emotional or behavioral disorders can begin in young children and continue through adulthood.
    a. early identification and intervention can prevent emotional or behavioral disorders and can reduce the impact of these disorders
    b. transitional programming can help provide more positive outcomes for adolescents and adults with emotional or behavioral disorders

14. In order to provide more effective interventions, family-centered approaches such as wrap-around programming are being utilized for students with emotional or behavioral disorders.

Application Exercises & Project Suggestions
1. Ask two teachers to share their techniques for effective behavior management. Note if either of them use token economies.
2. Visit a program for emotional or behavioral disordered students. Note the conceptual models that you see being implemented.

InfoTrac® Activity Suggestions

Activity 7.1: Classroom arrangement
This article suggests strategies for classroom arrangement to help with the management of behavior.

1. Locate and read **"So Much to do, so Little Time "** By Mary Rose in *Instructor*.

_____

_____

_____

2. Discuss the suggestions in the article that you feel are most important for the management of a classroom.

_____

_____

_____

3. Which activities deal directly with students?

_____

_____

_____

4. Which activities deal with teacher workspace organization?

_____

_____

_____

Activity 7.2: Social Skills Training

This article examined the importance of social skills training for students with emotional or behavioral disorders.

1. Locate and read **"Effective School-Based Mental Health Interventions: Advancing the Social Skills Training Paradigm"** by Steven Evans, Jennifer Axelrod, and Jennifer Sapia in *Journal of School Health*.

2. List three outcomes research has indicated are tied to social impairment.

_____

_____

_____

3. Discuss four ways social skills interventions can be improved.

_____

_____

_____

InfoTrac® Article Suggestions:

- Bennett, K., & Offord, D. (2001). Screening for conduct problems: Does the predictive accuracy of conduct disorder symptoms improve with age? <u>Journal of the American Academy of Child and Adolescent Psychiatry</u>, <u>40</u>, 1418.
- Findling, R., Short, E., & Manos, M.(2001). Developmental aspects of psychostimulant treatment in children and adolescents with attention-deficit/hyperactivity disorder. <u>Journal of the American Academy of Child and Adolescent Psychiatry</u>, <u>40</u>, 1441-1448.

Key Terms

Define each:

mentally ill_____

emotional of behavioral disorders_____

Tourette's syndrome_____

emotional disturbance_____

socially maladjusted_____

conduct disorders _____

clinically derived classification systems_____

statistically derived classification systems_____

externalizing disorders_____

internalizing disorders_____

child maltreatment_____

positive behavioral support_____

primary prevention_____

secondary prevention_____

tertiary prevention_____

person-centered planning_____

strength-based assessment_____

functional behavioral assessment_____

behavioral intervention plan_____

time management_____

transition management_____

proximity and movement management_____

classroom arrangement_____

classroom ambience_____

effective instructional cycle_____

mnemonic strategies_____

self-monitoring strategies_____

curriculum-based measurement_____

content enhancement_____

social skills training_____

interpersonal problem solving_____

conflict resolution_____

crisis prevention and management programs_____

wraparound plan_____

family-centered approach_____

systems of care model_____

CHAPTER SEVEN: PERSONS WITH EMOTIONAL OR BEHAVIORAL DISORDERS
Practice Test

True or False

1. Prevalence estimates of students with emotional or behavioral disorders vary due to conflicting definitions and a lack of consensus concerning what is meant by acceptable behavior. _____

2. Problematic behavior can be of a transient nature. _____

3. Students with socially maladjusted behavior are included in the federal definition for emotional or behavioral disorders. _____

4. Studies have shown that as the number of risk factors increase, so do the chances of negative outcomes for students with emotional or behavioral disorders. _____

5. Early research suggested that an infant's temperament had no effects on the development of an emotional or behavioral disorder. _____

6. Biological and environmental factors act independently in emotional or behavioral disorders.

   _____

7. Proactive measures for behavior change rely on prevention rather than reaction. _____

8. One of the most outstanding characteristics of students with emotional or behavioral disorders is their inability to maintain friendships. _____

9. PL 105-17 requires a behavioral intervention plan be developed for each student who exhibits problematic behaviors. _____

10. The presence of emotional or behavioral disorders is an indicator of later school failure.

   _____

Multiple Choice

1. All of the following are considered dimensions of behavior except
   a. frequency of a behavior occurring
   b. intensity of the behavior
   c. number of friends
   d. duration of the behavior

2. An example of a clinically derived classification system for students with emotional or behavioral disorder is
   a. WISC –III
   b. Quay and Peterson's Revised Behavior Problem Checklist
   c. DSM-IV-TR
   d. Stanford-Binet

3. The Council for Children with Behavior Disorders was formed in
    a. 1964
    b. 1975
    c. 1960
    d. 1990

4. Which of the following are attributes of resilient children?
    a. social competency
    b. excellent problem-solving skills
    c. independence
    d. all of the above

5. An example of a tertiary prevention method is
    a. social skills training
    b. token economies
    c. grouping students who are at-risk
    d. none of the above

6. Which of the following is an example of a transition time?
    a. going to the lunchroom
    b. changing from a math lesson to the reading lesson
    c. raising your hand
    d. a and b
    e. a and c

7. Characteristics of a difficult temperament are
    a. frequent irritability
    b. irregular patterns of sleeping and eating
    c. highly emotional behavior
    d. all of the above

8. Which of the following statements is true concerning the intelligence level of students with emotional or behavioral disorders?
    a. Most students score in the above average range of intelligence.
    b. Most students score at least 2 deviations from the average range of intelligence.
    c. Most students score in the low-average range of intelligence.

9. Research has shown
    a. girls are more likely to display internalizing behaviors
    b. girls are more likely to display externalizing behaviors
    c. there is no research on female behavior patterns
    d. none of the above

10. Assessment of students with emotional or behavioral disorders should
    a. rely only on the opinion of classroom teachers
    b. rely only on the results of psychologists' tests
    c. rely on information from a variety of sources from within the school and within the student's family.

Matching

Classroom ambience	content enhancement
Conflict resolution	behavioral model
Mentally ill	

1. Graphic organizers, study guides, and content diagrams are examples of _____.
2. The feeling one gets when entering a classroom is _____.
3. Programs that not only teach problem-solving skills but also teach negotiation and mediation skills are called _____.
4. The conceptual model that advocates all behavior is learned is called

   _____.

5. A term used by people outside the field of special education for people with emotional or behavioral disorders. _____

Chapter Seven: Persons with Emotional or Behavioral Disorders
Practice Test Answer Key

True or False
1. True.
2. True.
3. False. Students with socially maladjusted behaviors are excluded from the federal definition.
4. True.
5. False. Early research suggested that an infant's temperament had effects on the development of emotional or behavioral disorders.
6. False. Biological and environmental factors act concurrently in emotional and behavioral disorders.
7. True.
8. True.
9. True.
10. True.

Multiple Choice
1. C
2. C
3. A
4. D
5. B
6. D
7. D
8. C
9. A
10. C

Matching
1. Content enhancement
2. Classroom ambience
3. Conflict resolution
4. Behavioral model
5. Mentally ill

Check Your Understanding ⇨ **See textbook page 308**
Answer Key

1. **Explain why each of the following factors should be taken into consideration when defining emotional or behavioral disorders:**
Dimensions of behavior (frequency, intensity, duration, age-appropriateness):
The dimensions of behavior need to be taken into consideration due to the developmental appropriateness of the behavior being displayed.
Disturbed versus disturbing behavior:
Disturbing behavior can be deemed appropriate at a certain time while inappropriate at others; however, disturbed behavior is habitual and considered inappropriate in all settings.
Transient nature of problematic behavior:
Transient behavior may occur during a difficult period in an individual's life then disappear when the period ends; problematic behavior persists.
Typical versus atypical behavior:
Typical behaviors are age and developmentally appropriate whereas atypical behaviors are unusual behaviors that are different from expectations for age and development.
Variability in cultural and social standards of behavior:
The variability of cultural and societal norms leads to the lack of acceptance of some behaviors.

2. **Why is the federal definition of emotional disturbance controversial? How does this definition differ from the one proposed by the Mental Health and Special Education Coalition? Discuss the pros and cons of each definition.**
The exclusion of "socially maladjusted" children from the federal definition has caused great controversy. Other terms within the federal definition have been cited as being too narrow in their interpretation. The definition proposed by the Mental Health and Special Education coalition is inclusive of conduct-disordered children and offers a broader view of emotional and behavioral disorders. While the federal definition offers a restricted interpretation of emotional and behavioral disorders, the new definition may be too broad in its definition.

3. **Compare and contrast clinically and statistically derived classification systems. Give examples of each.**
Clinically derived classification systems group behaviors into categories and use derived criteria to make diagnosis. Statistically derived classification systems are based on patterns of disordered behavior from which standards of eligibility are determined. The most commonly used clinical system is DSM-IV-TR. Another statistical system is the Revised Behavior Problem Checklist.

4. **Define externalizing and internalizing disorders. Give an example of behaviors reflecting each of these two dimensions.**
Externalizing behaviors are characterized by "acting out" – disruptive, aggressive behavior – such as throwing a chair across the room. Internalizing behaviors are characterized by withdrawal and depression such as attempted suicide.

5. **Describe various conceptual models in the field of emotional and behavioral disorders.**
The behavioral model is based upon the assumption that behavior is learned thus inappropriate behavior is learned and reinforced through the environment. The psychoanalytic model is based on the work of Freud that assumes disturbed behavior is a result of underlying conflicts that must be resolved. The psychoeducational model has its basis in the unconscious goals the individual wants to attain by their behavior. Teachers aim at helping the child realize their mistaken goal. In the ecological model, the student is seen as being influenced by all the components of their social surroundings. The humanistic model stresses the ability of the individual to generate their own solutions to their problems. The biogenic model assumes disturbing behaviors are a result of physiological flaws.

6. **List four causes of, and risk factors associated with, emotional or behavioral disorders.**

Several risk factors are associated with emotional and behavioral disorders. These include environmental factors such as parental discord, a parent with mental illness, overcrowding in the home, early maternal infection, neglect, and abuse.

7. **How does a positive behavioral support model differ from traditional disciplinary methods?**

The positive behavioral support model advocates proactive measures rather than the reactive measures of traditional disciplinary measures. Positive support looks at preventing the occurrence of the behavior.

8. **What are some of the significant learning, social, and language/communication characteristics of children and youth with emotional or behavioral disorders?**

Research has shown that many students with emotional and behavior disorders score in the low-average range of intelligence. However, co-existing factors such as learning disabilities add to the learning problems for these students. The inability to make and maintain friendships stands out as a social characteristic. Students with emotional and behavioral disorders have problems with using language in the social context.

9. **List five strategies that are typically used to assess students with emotional and behavioral disorders.**

Strategies used for students include: interviews with the student, parents, and teachers; medical evaluations; standardized norm-referenced tests; functional behavioral assessments; and observations in natural settings.

10. **What is functional behavioral assessment?**

Functional behavioral assessments take into accounting that problematic behaviors occur for many reasons: physiological factors, classroom environmental factors and curriculum and instructional factors. This type of assessment examines the variables that precede and follow the inappropriate behavior in order to form positive behavior supports.

11. **Describe how you would use the following intervention strategies with students with emotional or behavioral disorders: social skills training; interpersonal problem solving and conflict resolution; counseling and school health services; crisis prevention and management programs**

One outstanding feature of students with emotional or behavioral disorders is their inability to maintain friendships. Social skills training uses direct instruction to teach appropriate social behaviors. Interpersonal problem solving and conflict resolution teaches students the thinking skills necessary to resolve interpersonal conflicts and handle peer pressure. Counseling and school health services need to be utilized to help students discuss their problems and handle medication administration. Crisis prevention and management programs act as proactive measures educators can use to address student violent behaviors.

12. **How can a teacher manipulate the physical environment to assist students with and without emotional or behavioral disorders?**

A number of classroom environmental variables can be used by the teacher to promote positive interactions: time management skills for teachers as well as students help to minimize disruptions; transition management helps students move from one activity to another thus structuring the transition time; and classroom arrangement and inviting atmosphere add to a feeling of belonging in the classroom.

13. **List five academic and instruction interventions that are more effective with pupils with emotional or behavioral disorders.**

Mnemonic strategies, self-monitoring strategies, curriculum-based measurement, content enhancers and effective instructional cycles.

14. **Provide an argument for providing early intervention services for students who have, or who are at risk for developing, emotional or behavioral disorders**

Research has shown that young children who display overly aggressive behavior and other inappropriate behaviors do not outgrow them but tend to intensify the dimension of their behaviors as they grow older. These behaviors can be precursors of addictions as well as other anti-social behaviors.

15. **What does research say about the long-term outcomes for students with emotional or behavioral disorders ?**

Research shows primarily negative outcomes for students with emotional and behavioral problems. These include high drop-out rates, incarceration, and addiction.

16. **What issues need to be considered when planning for transition of adolescents with emotional or behavioral disorders?**

Transition planning for students with behavioral and emotional disorders needs to span their lifetime. Issues of employment, community integration, independent living skills and educational opportunities need to be addressed.

CHAPTER EIGHT
PERSONS WHO ARE GIFTED AND TALENTED

Overview of Persons who are Gifted and Talented
Chapter Eight is an overview of the field of education for gifted and talented students. The author presents various definitions of gifted and talented. Also a brief history of the field of education of the gifted and talented is provided. Characteristics of children who are gifted and talented are described as well as educational interventions for this population of children is provided. Educational service delivery options are reviewed and future issues concerning this field of exceptionality are discussed.

Chapter Key Points
- Terman conducted the first long term study of children who are gifted and talented
- The Marland Report expanded the number of categories of children who are considered gifted.
- The causes of giftedness are both genetic and environmental.
- Strategies to assist children who are gifted and talented include curriculum compacting, differentiating the curriculum, mentorships, cluster grouping, enrichment, and self-contained service options.
- Assessment of children who are gifted and talented should include both informal and formal measures.
- Issues in the field of gifted and talented include equity, full inclusion, and striving for world class standards.

Focus and Reflect
Discuss two causes of giftedness.

_____

_____

_____

Discuss the six aspects of giftedness as defined in the Marland Report.

_____

_____

_____

Discuss Renzulli'sThree Ring model of giftedness.

_____

_____

_____

Discuss three accleration options for students who are gifted and talented.

_____

_____

_____

Chapter Guided Review

1. Defining giftedness
    a. gifted often equated with high intelligence
    b. Marland Report-specified six areas of giftedness (general intellectual ability, specific academic aptitude, creative or productive thinking, leadership ability, visual and performing arts, and psychomotor ability)
    c. Renzulli-Three Ring model of giftedness consisting of above average intellectual abilities, creativity, and task commitment
    d. Features of program for children who are gifted and talented-each state establishes its own definition; gifted included as a category of exceptionality (in some states); specifics about area of giftedness lead to appropriate services; gifted and talented focuses on high levels of performance; gifted in all ethnic and racial groups

2. Assessing gifted and talented
    a. informal assessment- jot downs about students
    b. formal assessment-Pfeiffer-Jarosewich Gifted Rating Scales, Wechsler Intelligence Scale for Children-Third Edition, Stanford-Binet-Fourth Edition
    c. off-level testing-Woodcock-Johnson-III Tests of Achievement, Scholastic Aptitude Test
    d. creativity-test by E. Paul Torrance and Frank Williams
    e. leadership-assessment through portfolios
    f. artistic skills-assessment through portfolio and performance
    g. school district's plan for assessment of gifted children-ongoing, written plan, can occur any time, non-biased, includes multiple measures, informed consent

3. Differences among children who are gifted and talented
    a. IQ difference
    b. Varying levels of potential and performance

4. A brief history of the field of gifted and talented education
    a. The first half of the twentieth century: pioneering the field-Terman's first longitudinal Study of gifted children; refuting the concept of early ripe/early rot; Leta Hollingworth study of highly gifted children
    b. The 1950s, 1960s, and 1970s: Establishing foundations for the field-Guilford-multiple Intelligences; founding of the National Association for Gifted Children; launching of Sputnik I starts emphasis in the areas of science and math; differential education initiated; Marland Report broadens definition of giftedness; no national mandate for gifted and talented children in P. L. 94-142.
    c. The 1980s and 1990s: The field matures and provides focus for school reform-Gardner and Sternberg's work concerning multiple intelligences; Gardner-linguistic, logical-mathematical, spatial, bodily-kinesthetic, musical, interpersonal, intrapersonal; Sternberg-practical, creative, and executive intelligences; *A Nation at Risk* published; Office of Gifted and Talented Education established; National Research Center on Gifted and Talented-research for policy decisions

5. Prevalence of giftedness and talent
    a. U. S. Department of Education-6% of school population are gifted
    b. 3-5% of school-age population-gifted-most estimates

6. Etiology of gifted and talented
    a. genetic patterns and environment-key roles
    b. intelligence not fixed at birth
    c. vital role of early stimulation in ability to learn
    d. parents and educators-significant roles in increasing capacity to learn

7. Characteristics of persons who are gifted and talented
    a. perform childhood tasks ahead of schedule-talk early, read before entering school, exceptional memories
    b. exceptional talent in one or more specific academic areas
    c. creativity-strong imagination, risk takers, tolerance of ambiguity
    d. leadership-initiate activities, plans to reach goals
    e. visual and performing arts-exceptional work in this area

8. Educational considerations
    a. no or minor modifications made by regular education teachers to meet needs of gifted learners
    b. differentiation-used to meet the different abilities of all students; uses pre-assessment of child's knowledge and skills
    c. curriculum compacting-time spent on academic subjects is telescoped or reduced to allow students to make continuous progress; frequently done in language arts and math
    d. higher-level thinking and problem solving-team projects and individual opportunities for higher level thinking strategies
    e. flexible grouping-grouping by interests, needs, and abilities
    f. cluster grouping-placing five or more students with similar needs and abilities with one teacher
    g. pacing instruction-a faster pace of instruction for individuals who are gifted and talented
    h. creativity-stresses originality, fluency, flexibility, and elaboration; need opportunities to develop talents in a risk-free learning environment

9. Service delivery options
    a. gifted resource services-provided to gifted children in a pull out program
    b. acceleration-one content area; full year acceleration; Advanced Placement classes in high school
    c. independent study-independent and in-depth study of an area of interest
    d. honors and advanced placement courses-honors courses include advanced content; Advanced Placement courses can earn college credit
    e. mentorships-older expert working with younger and talented individual in an area of mutual interest
    f. self-contained classes and special schools-North Carolina School of Math and Science, North Carolina School of the Performing Arts
    g. summer and Saturday programs-Summer Ventures, Duke Talent Identification Program
    h. competitions-provides motivation and challenge for gifted and talented children

10. Services for young children who are gifted and talented
    a. gifts of young children overlooked
    b. early identification essential
    c. early admission to kindergarten or first grade
    d. play as important as academics

11. Adolescents and adults who are gifted and talented
    a. adolescence-fitting in, frequent lack of appropriately challenging instruction career choices established early
    b. 10-20% of high school dropouts are gifted and talented
    c. MENSA for gifted adults

12. Family issues
    a. family support vital for achievement and accomplishment
    b. families benefit from state and national organizations for the gifted and talented

13. Issues of diversity
    a. students with gifts and talents and disabilities-one diagnosis masks needs of second disability; gifted/talented and learning disabled; blending instructional strategies for compensating for disability and emphasizing strengths
    b. girls who are gifted-underrepresented gifted population, unequal educational opportunities, parental expectations, lower, sex-role stereotyping; offer help in confidence, self-esteem, assertiveness
    c. identifying and serving children from diverse backgrounds-culturally diverse students underrepresented in programs for children who are gifted and talented; poverty masks giftedness; issues: test bias, conflicting cultural values, and faulty referral policies

14. Technology and persons who are gifted and talented
    a. virtual high schools and universities
    b. e-mail
    c. teleconferencing
    d. Internet
    e. lessens isolation of children who are gifted and talented

15. Trends, issues, and controversies
    a. striving for world-class standards-need to challenge gifted and talented students; United States math and science scores lowest among forty-one countries
    b. full inclusion-often restrictive for gifted and talented individuals; need a full range of program options to meet needs of students
    c. services for gifted students instead of the gifted program-develop services to match the needs of interests of students
    d. equity and excellence-opportunities for all students to achieve excellence

Application Exercises & Project Suggestions

1. Observe in a self-contained magnet school for students who are gifted and talented. List the academic challenges which students find in such a situation.
2. Interview a student in a program for the visual and performing arts. What types of gifts and talents does this student exhibit?
3. Discuss three positives and three negatives concerning educating children who are gifted and talented in an inclusive classroom.

InfoTrac® Activity Suggestions

Activity 8.1: Gifted and Talented
This activity is based on an article concerning a young child who is gifted and talented. The article provides insights into creativity and imagination that is eventually shared by the entire class.

1. Locate and read **"Mr. Different: Sometimes It Takes Time To See the Unusual Child is Gifted"** by Diane Butcher found in *Instructor*.

2. What was Shaun's planet like?

_____

_____

3. How did Shaun's teacher respond to his creative thinking?

_____

_____

_____

4. How did Shaun's creativity help others in the class to expand their thinking skills?

_____

_____

_____

Activity 8.2: Magnet high schools
This activity focuses on the rigors of an inner city magnet school that stresses high academic standards.

1. Locate and read **"Higher Standards"** found in *U.S. News and World Report*.

_____

_____

_____

2. What were two objectives of the Men of Vision.

_____

_____

_____

3. Discuss two strategies used by Renaissance High School concerning the implementation of high academic standards.

_____

_____

_____

4. Discuss the work ethic that seems to be prevalent in the students and faculty at Renaissance High School. Does this work ethic seem to be beneficial to the students?

_____

_____

_____

InfoTrac® Article Suggestions
- Plucker, J., & Stocking, V. (2001). Looking outside and inside: Self-concept development of gifted adolescents. Exceptional Children, 67, 535-539.
- Clark, G., & Zimmerman, E. (1998). Nurturing the arts in programs for gifted and talented students. Phi Delta Kappan, 79, 747-752.

Key Terms

Define each:

gifted and talented_____

off-level testing_____

creativity_____

differential education_____

preassessment_____

curriculum compacting_____

flexible grouping_____

cooperative learning_____

cluster grouping_____

acceleration_____

enrichment_____

mentor_____

magnet high schools_____

twice exceptional_____

CHAPTER EIGHT: PERSONS WHO ARE GIFTED AND TALENTED
Practice Test

True or False
1. Most gifted children are hyperactive._____

2. Terman conducted the first long term study of gifted children._____

3. Off-level testing uses instruments that remove the learning ceiling._____

4. Tests by E. Paul Torrance and Frank Williams are used to assess the visual and performing

    arts._____

5. Guilford thought that intelligence was unitary trait._____

6. Differential education is a curriculum which allows gifted students to learn at appropriate

    levels._____

7. The impact of the launching of Sputnik had no impact on the educational curriculum in the

    United States._____

8. *A Nation At Risk* found that 50% of the school-age population were not performing up to their

    potential._____

Multiple Choice
1. Characteristics of gifted children include
    a. creativity.
    b. talent in one or more academic areas.
    c. leadership characteristics.
    d. all of the above.

2. Differentiation means:
    a. all children are treated alike
    b. children are offered a curriculum that meets their needs.
    c. All children are served in inclusive settings.
    d. None of the above.

3. Early ripe, early rot
    a. was proven true.
    b. relates to fruits and vegetables.
    c. was proven incorrect in the Terman study.
    d. was an early theory concerning the life progression of gifted children.

4. Preassessment means:
    a. finding where children are currently functioning in certain academic areas.
    b. starting at the same point in teaching all children.
    c. only done by parents.
    d. none of the above.

5. Acceleration includes:
    a. advanced classes in certain academic areas.
    b. honors classes.
    c. grade skipping.
    d. all of the above.

6. Mentorships:
    a. involve an older expert in the field.
    b. emphasizes the gifted child's area of interest.
    c. are not favored by schools.
    d. are only done in the area of the performing arts.

7. The Three Ring model by Renzulli stresses:
    a. creativity.
    b. above average intellectual abilities.
    c. task commitment.
    d. performing arts.

8. Which of the following areas did the Marland Report consider categories of giftedness:
    a. intellectual ability.
    b. creative thinking.
    c. specific academic aptitude.
    d. all of the above.

9. Leadership is:
    a. assessed by portfolios.
    b. can be demonstrated in one area.
    c. is easy to identify.
    d. none of the above.

10. Guilford:
    a. identified intelligence as a unitary trait.
    b. identified one hundred and twenty aspects of intelligence.
    c. initiated a national report on giftedness.
    d. none of the above.

Matching

1. early ripe, early rot
2. jot downs
3. Terman
4. acceleration
5. Renzulli's Three Ring Model
6. causes of giftedness
7. E. Paul Torrance
8. mentorship
9. curriculum compacting
10. Hollingworth

a. above average ability, creativity, task commitment
b. created measures to assess creativity
c. conducted a study of extremely gifted children
d. an informal way of assessing children who are gifted and talented
e. one example is grade skipping
f. an early theory concerning the development of children who are gifted and talented
g. time spent on academic subjects is telescoped
h. doing work with an expert in a field of interest
i. an interaction of heredity and environmental stimulation
j. conducted first long term study of gifted children

Chapter 8: Persons who are Gifted and Talented
Practice Test Answer Key

True or False
1. False. Gifted children are active but the activity is focused, directed, and intense.
2. True
3. True
4. False. Tests by E. Paul Torrance and Frank Williams are used to assess creativity.
5. False. Guilford identified one hundred and twenty different kinds of intelligence
6. True
7. False. The launching of Sputnik caused the United States to stress mathematics and science in educational curricula.
8. True

Multiple Choice
1. D
2. B
3. C and D
4. A
5. D
6. A and B
7. A, B, and C
8. D
9. A and B
10. B

Matching
1. F
2. D
3. J
4. E
5. A
6. I
7. B
8. H
9. G
10. C

Check Your Understanding ⇨See textbook page 358
Answer Key

1. How are children with gifts and talents identified?
Teacher, parent, and peer nomination help in the identification of children who are gifted. Test of intelligence are used to identify the intellectual level of gifted students. Off-level tests like the Scholastic Aptitude Test and the Woodcock-Johnson III help to identify the achievement levels of students. Informal assessments like teacher recommendations and jot-downs also are helpful in identifying gifted children.

2. Why is the assessment of giftedness a difficult procedure?
Assessment of giftedness is difficult because state guidelines vary and the concept of giftedness takes into account such a wide variety of talents.

3. How has society's view and understanding of children with gifts and talents changed during the past century?
In the 1920s Terman conducted a long term study of children who were gifted. He found that the early ripe/early rot theory of intelligence was a myth. Hollingworth found that intelligence was influenced by both heredity and environment. In the 1950s –1970s, the field of gifted education developed a greater concept of what constitutes giftedness. Guildford identified 120 different types of intelligence. The Marland Report noted six areas of giftedness. Sputnik encouraged a greater emphasis on science and math. Differential education stressed the concept of a curriculum designed to meet the child's needs. In the 1980s and 1990s, Gardner and Sternberg identified seven intelligences that included linguistic, logical, mathematical, spatial, bodily-kinesthetic, musical, interpersonal, and intrapersonal. Also the Office of Gifted and Talented Education was created at the federal level. The National Research Center on Gifted and Talented conducts research to help in policy decisions.

4. The etiology of giftedness is seen as the commingling or interaction of what variables?
Giftedness is the result of the interaction of genetic patterns and environmental stimulation.

5. Identify five characteristics typically associated with individuals considered gifted and talented.
Five characteristics often associated with individuals who are gifted and talented are: performance of childhood tasks ahead of schedule, a talent in one or more specific academic area, creative, often exhibits leadership characteristics, and exceptional talent in art, music, dance and drama

6. Describe the various delivery models that are frequently used to meet the cognitive and social-emotional needs of children who are gifted and talented.
The service delivery models in the area of gifted and talented are resource rooms where gifted children can work with each other part of the time, acceleration where gifted and talented move ahead in certain subjects (accelerated classes, honors classes, and Advance Placement classes)or a whole year, independent and in-depth exploration of certain subjects, mentorships with an adult in a field of study, self-contained classes, special schools, competitions, Saturday programs, and summer programs.

7. Define the following terms: curriculum differentiation, pre-assessment, curriculum compacting, flexible grouping, and pacing.
Curriculum differentiation is a changing of the curriculum to meet the specific needs of children. The learning and pace ceilings are removed. Pre-assessment is determining the current functioning of students in various academic areas. Pre-assessment allows teacher to differentiate learning for students and keep it interesting. Curriculum compacting is an instructional procedure where the time spent on academics is reduced to allow progress at the student's level. Flexible grouping is the grouping of students by their interests, needs, and

abilities. Flexible grouping is required to meet the needs of all students. Pacing is the term used to acquire skills. Gifted and talented children learn at a much faster pace. Accelerated pacing must be linked to complex content and challenging learning experiences.

8. Distinguish between the concepts of acceleration and enrichment.

Acceleration is telescoping the curriculum for gifted and talented children who learn at a faster pace. This includes skipping a grade, advanced work in certain subjects, honors classes, and Advanced Placement classes. Enrichment allows gifted and talented students to stay in a regular classroom but provides resource room services or special activities to meet the learning needs of these children.

9. List five early indicators of gifts and talents.

Five early indicators of gifts and talents are these children speak in sentences before age mates, acquire number concepts sooner, often are musically talented demonstrate artwork which is similar to someone who is older, have excellent memories, and assume leadership roles.

10. What challenges do families of children who are gifted and talented frequently encounter?

Parents are vital in the child's achievement and accomplishment. Parents often spend extra time securing services for their children. Gifted and talented children often take music lessons, go to summer enrichment programs, and travel. All of these activities often occur at the parents' expense in terms of time and finances.

11. Why are some groups of children underrepresented in programs for students who are gifted and talented?

Girls and children from diverse cultures seem to be underrepresented in programs for gifted and talented children. Girls need for adults to have high expectations, believe in their local abilities, provide acceleration in science and math, assist in developing long-term career goals, discourage sexist curriculum, attitudes, and communication, and provide role models. Children from diverse backgrounds need cultural sensitivity in the identification process, establishing support services, greater community and family involvement, early identification, and alternative assessment practices in identification for gifted and talented programs.

12. How can technology be used to enhance learning opportunities for students with gifts and talents?

Technology makes resources available to everyone. This includes Internet, virtual high schools, and virtual universities. Students can participate in computer simulated activities. Technology is used to lessen the isolation of children who are gifted and talented and bring them in contact with others who have similar interests.

13. Why do some educators believe that full inclusion is not the best option for students who are gifted and talented?

Many teachers only make slight modification for gifted and talented children in the regular classroom. For many children who are gifted and talented, the least restrictive environment may be a self-contained class or magnet school. There are a number of self-contained high schools that focus on performing arts or math and science.

CHAPTER NINE
PERSONS WITH SPEECH AND LANGUAGE DISORDERS

Overview of Persons with Speech and Language Disorders
This chapter is an overview of various speech and language disorders. Speech disorders and language disorders are defined and causes for each are presented. Further various intervention strategies are proposed to help children and adults with speech and language disorders. Finally, augmentative or alternative communication interventions are discussed.

Chapter Key Points
- Speech disorders includes disorders in articulation, phonation and resonance, and fluency.
- Language is governed by five rules that include phonology, morphology, syntax, semantics, and pragmatics.
- Speech and language problems results from functional or organic causes.
- Family centered rehabilitation strategies represent best practices for families and professionals in working with children with speech and language disorders.
- Augmentative or alternative communication strategies offer supportive intervention alternatives for children with severe speech disabilities.

Focus and Reflect
Discuss the use of a communication board.

_____

_____

_____

Discuss two helpful ways to interact with individuals who stutter.

_____

_____

_____

Discuss the meaning of pragmatics.

_____

_____

_____

Discuss three educational implications for central auditory processing disorders.

_____

_____

_____

Chapter Guided Review

1. Defining speech and language disorders
   a. defined in IDEA under special education and related services
   b. provision of speech and language disorders varies from state to state
2. Classifying speech and language disorders
   a. speech disorders – articulation disorders (omissions, substitutions and distortions), voice disorders (pitch, loudness, and quality), fluency disorders (stuttering and cluttering)
   b. language disorders – language behaviors (listening, speaking, reading and writing); language disorders have pervasive negative effects on the educational process
   c. deficits in language systems: phonology, morphology, syntax, semantics and pragmatics
   d. central auditory processing disorder – problems in processing sound not attributed to hearing loss or intellectual capacity; affects transmission, analysis, organization, storage, retrieval and use of sound information
   e. apraxia of speech – caused by oral-motor difficulty and limitations of expression
3. Historical perspectives
   a. historic reactions towards individuals with disabilities – rejection, objects of pity and a source of humor
   b. historical titles of therapist – speech correctionists, speech specialists, speech teachers; today expanded role of speech and language pathologist
4. Prevalence of speech and language disorders
   a. 20% of children receiving special education are receiving services for speech and hearing disorders
   b. 1 in 10 people in US has a speech and language disorder
5. Etiology of speech and language disorders
   a. functional etiologies – no obvious physical basis (ex. environmental stress)
   b. organic etiologies – physiological deficit (cleft palate)
   c. congenital disorders – existing at birth
   d. acquired disorders – results of injury, disease, environment
   e. classifications by onset, severity, behavioral characteristics
   f. etiologies of communication disorders – congenital malformations, prenatal injury, tumor, problems in central nervous system, brain and speech mechanism; traumatic brain injury and meningitis
6. Prevention of speech and language disorders
   a. developmental language delay – slow to develop adequate vocabulary and grammar
   b. early intervention critical in area of developmental language delay
   c. hearing loss results in delays in language, education, and performance
7. Characteristics of speech and language disorders
   a. expressive language deficits – grammar, syntax, fluency, vocabulary, and repetition
   b. receptive language deficits – response, abstraction, retention, and recall
   c. intelligence speech and basis of adult grammar developed before age 4; all speech sounds can be produced by age 8
8. Assessing speech and language disorders
   a. case history – family directed assessment to determine needs, concerns, resources, and priorities
   b. team approach - involves teachers, audiologists, speech pathologists, neurologists, physicians, parents and learning disability specialists
   c. central auditory processing disorder – listening difficulties in many classroom situations
   d. evaluate physical, educational, communicative abilities, psychological and social status
   e. Goldman-Fristoe Test of Articulation – measure of articulation terms of consonants in initial, middle, and final positions

f. Informal measures – conversational sampling of speech
g. Brigance Diagnostic Inventory of Early Development – used for prelinguistic communicative behaviors
h. Assessing communication disorders – screening, referral, eligibility determination, program planning, program monitoring, program evaluation
9. Educational considerations
   a. Minority of children with speech and language disorders served in general classroom
   b. Responsibilities of the speech and language pathologist – prevention of speech and language disorders, identification of children in need of services, IEP/IFSP development, and coordinates service delivery to students
10. Services for young children with speech and language disorders
   a. the younger the child, the more positive the outlook for remediation strategies
   b. all states serve children 0-5 years of age
   c. developmental rating scales- analyze communication-promoting behaviors between a child and his/her caregiver
   d. evaluation of language skills- include adaptive behavior scales, parent interventions, informal language sampling
11. Adolescents and adults with speech and language disorders
   a. problems exhibited by children – searching for own identity, independence, group loyalty compounded by communication problems
12. Family issues
   a. medical model of assessment – diagnosis by committee, reports filled with technical jargon
   b. contemporary educational model of assessment – child-centered treatment of communication disorders
   c. best practice – include families and children in the assessment process
13. Issues of diversity
   a. numbers of children with dialectical, cultural, or regional variations of speech and language are increasing in numbers
   b. varieties of spoken English reflect person's environment
   c. care not to label communication difference as a communication disorder
   d. dialect is a variation of a symbol system shared by regional, social, or ethnic factors
14. Technology and persons with speech and language disorders
   a. augmentative or alternative communication – symbols, aids, strategies and techniques used to enhance the communication process
   b. communication board – choices, real items, pictures of items, symbols of items
   c. electronic AAC devices – uses voice (CheapTalk, DynaVox)
   d. frequency modulated systems – transmission of a signal from a teacher's microphone to a student's receiver; types include self-contained and sound field systems
15. Trends, issues, and controversies
   a. early intervention – urgent need in the area of speech and language disorders
   b. medication and educational assessment and intervention strategies – may lead to reduction in incidence of some types of speech and language problems
   c. family –centered approach – families are partners in the rehabilitation process
   d. technology – holds promise for individuals and families dealing with speech and language disorders

Application Exercises & Project Suggestions

1. Visit a speech and language pathologist and observe a therapy session. Discuss two strategies he/she used with a child during the therapy session.
2. Interview parents of children with a cleft palate. Report on their experiences concerning their child's surgeries and accompanying therapies.
3. Discuss two augmentative and alternative communication strategies.

InfoTrac® Activity Suggestions

Activity 9.1: Gene mutation as a cause of speech and language disorder
This article discusses the impact on one family of a gene mutation as a cause of speech and language disorders.

1. Locate and read **"Gene Change Speaks to Language Malady"** by B. Bower in *Science News*.

2. Discuss three speech and language problems that the family in the article experienced as a result of a gene mutation.

_____

_____

_____

3. Discuss the major finding of the article concerning a mutation in a gene can causes specific speech and language problems.

_____

_____

_____

4. Do you believe that genes actually map out grammar circuits in the brain?

_____

_____

_____

Activity 9.2: Speech and language therapy
This article reviews the need for additional speech and language therapy for young children experiencing neurodevelopmental impairments.

1. Locate and read **"Treating Children with Speech and Language Impairments: Six hours of Therapy is Not Enough"** by James Law and Gina Conti-Ramsden in the *British Medical Journal.*

2. What percentage of children under the age of five have developmental impairments of speech and language?

_____

_____

_____

3. What are the benefits of speech and language therapy for young children with developmental impairments?

_____

_____

_____

4. Do you think that six hours of speech and language therapy in twelve months is enough therapy? What might be the benefits of additional therapy time?

_____

_____

_____

InfoTrac Article Suggestions
- Levy, Y., Tennenbaurm, A., & Ornoy, A. (2000). Spontaneous language of children with specific neurological syndromes. Journal of Speech, Language and Hearing Research, 43, 351-353.
- Toppelberg, C., & Shapiro, T. (2000). Language disorders: A ten year research update review. Journal of the American Academy of Child and Adolescent Psychiatry, 39, 143-145.

Key Terms

Define each:

speech and language disorders_____

speech-language pathologist_____

communication disorders_____

articulation disorders_____

omissions_____

substitutions_____

distortions_____

voice disorders_____

phonation_____

vocal resonance_____

hypernasality_____

hyponasality_____

fluency disorders_____

stuttering_____

cluttering_____

language disorder_____

phonology_____

morphology_____

syntax_____

semantics_____

pragmatic_____

central auditory processing disorder (CAPA)_____

apraxia_____

functional_____

organic_____

aphasia_____

cleft lip_____

cleft palate_____

developmental language delay_____

oral language_____

receptive language_____

expressive language_____

family-directed assessment_____

language sample_____

prelinguistic_____

dialect_____

augmentative or alternative communication (AAC)_____

FM systems_____

personal FM systems_____

self-contained FM systems_____

Sound field FM systems_____

CHAPTER NINE: PERSONS WITH SPEECH AND LANGUAGE DISORDERS
Practice Test

True or False
1. Aphasia is the loss of speech resulting from stuttering._____

2. An example of a fluency disorder is stuttering._____

3. Hyponasality is an example of an articulation problem._____

4. Syntax is the rule system governing the order and combination of words to form sentences._____

5. Apraxia is comprised of both a speech disorder and a language disorder._____

6. Today, language specialists are called speech and language pathologists._____

7. The number of children receiving services for speech and hearing disorders is very small._____

8. A communication board is an example of a fm system._____

Multiple Choice
1. Causes of communication disorders include:
    a. aphasia.
    b. hearing impairments.
    c. speech and language problems.
    d. all of the above.

2. An example of an articulation disorder is:
    a. omission of sounds
    b. apraxia
    c. dyslexia
    d. none of the above

3. In working with individuals who stutter:
    a. ask them to stop and start over in what they were saying.
    b. be patient.
    c. seek professional intervention early.
    d. bring attention to their speech problem.

4. Phonology:
    a. is another word for syntax.
    b. is the use of sounds to create meaningful syllables and words.
    c. is the smallest meaningful unit of language.
    d. none of the above.

5. Central auditory processing disorders:
    a. are problems processing sounds.
    b. are caused by hearing impairments.
    c. are caused by mental retardation.
    d. all of the above.

6. Functional causes of speech and language disorders:
    a. have an obvious physical basis.
    b. have no obvious physical basis.
    c. are caused by injury.
    d. are caused by disease.

7. The critical period of language acquisition is:
    a. birth to two years.
    b. birth to ten years.
    c. birth to six years.
    d. none of the above.

8. Family directed assessment:
    a. focuses on information provided by families regarding needs, concerns, resources, priorities.
    b. is used in identifying a child's strengths and weaknesses.
    c. is used in determining necessary support services.
    d. all of the above.

9. Assessments in the area of speech include:
    a. Goldman-Fristoe Test of Articulation.
    b. Brigance Diagnostic Inventory of Early Development.
    c. Key Math.
    d. Wechsler Individual Achievement Test.

10. Assessment of children with communication disorders includes:
    a. screening.
    b. referral.
    c. determination of eligibility.
    d. program planning.
    e. program monitoring and evaluation.
    f. all of the above.
    g. none of the above.

Matching

1. stuttering _____
2. speech & language pathologist _____
3. Bliss symbols _____
4. dialect _____
5. aphasia _____
6. receptive language _____
7. substitution _____
8. pragmatics _____
9. voice quality problems _____
10. communication board _____

a. an articulation disorder
b. ability to understand what is meant by spoken communication
c. an example of augmentative or alternative communication
d. an example of phonation problems
e. current term for a language professional
f. a fluency disorder
g. symbology system option used on communication boards
h. variation of a symbol system used by a group of individuals
i. use of communication skills in social contexts
j. loss of speech and language as a result of a stroke or head injury

Chapter 9: Persons with Speech and Language Disorders
Practice Test Answer Key

True or False
1. False. Aphasia is the loss of speech resulting from brain injury or stroke.
2. True
3. False. Hyponasality is an example of a voice disorder problem.
4. True
5. True
6. True
7. False. The number of children receiving services for speech and hearing disorders is approximately twenty percent of children receiving special education services.
8. False. A communication board is an example of an augmentative or alternative communication system.

Multiple Choice
1. D
2. A
3. B and C
4. B
5. A
6. B
7. C
8. D
9. A and B
10. F

Matching
1. F
2. E
3. G
4. H
5. J
6. B
7. A
8. I
9. D
10. C

Check Your Understanding ⇨ See textbook pages 396-397
Answer Key

1. What are the two main categories of communication disorders?
The two main categories of communication disorders are speech and language disorders.

2. How does IDEA define speech and language disorders?
Speech and language disorders are defined in The Individuals with Disabilities Education Act (P. L. 105-17) as a communication disorder such as stuttering, impaired articulation, a language impairment, or voice impairment which adversely affects a child's educational performance.

3. List the three broad categories of speech disorders and give an example of each.
The three broad categories of speech disorders are articulation disorders (omissions, substitutions, and distortions), voice disorders (hypernasality and hyponasality), and fluency disorders (stuttering and cluttering).

4. Define language, and explain how it is different from speech.
Speech is the most common expression of language. It requires coordination of the neuromusculature of the breathing and voice-producing mechanisms and the integrity of the mouth or oral cavity. Language behaviors are grouped into listening, speaking, reading, and writing.

5. List several factors that cause or contribute to voice disorders.
Voice disorders result from disorders of the larynx and phonation qualities of pitch, loudness, and quality. Causes of voice disorders are colds, allergies, chemically induced irritation, vocally demanding activities, vocal nodules, and cleft palate.

6. At what age should a child be pronouncing all sounds correctly? What course of action should be taken if he or she is not?
By age eight a child should be pronouncing all of his/her sounds accurately. When a developmental language delay is noted, early educational and speech/language therapy should be initiated as soon as possible.

7. List the five rules that must be learned for successful language acquisition to occur.
Children must learn five basic sets of rules to use language. They learn these rules by listening to language around them. The sets of rules are:
(1) phonology (use of sounds to create meaningful syllables and words)
(2) morphology (dictates how the smallest meaningful units of language are combined into words)
(3) syntax (puts together a series of words and determines word order used in communication)
(4) semantics (how words are used meaningfully in communication)
(5) pragmatics (use of communication skills in social contexts)

8. Define central auditory processing disorder. What types of intervention strategies are most effective with this population?
Children with central auditory processing disorder process auditory input in a slow and inaccurate way. These children have a difficult time in many classroom situations. Some intervention strategies include selecting seating away from auditory or visual distractions, reducing visual and auditory distractions in the classroom, using ear plugs to block distracting noise, using a study carrel in the classroom, gaining the child's attention before speaking. Other strategies include speaking slowly and clearly, using simple and brief directions, giving directions in time ordered sequence, using visual aids and writing instruction, emphasizing key words, varying loudness in speaking, paraphrasing material, and avoid having the child listen and write at the same time.

9. Describe the evolution of the role of the speech-language pathologist during the twentieth century.

The first speech correction teachers were hired in 1910 in Chicago. From 1910 to 1950 speech interventionists include speech correctionists, speech specialists, or speech teachers. Eventually these professionals were titled speech therapists. As speech professionals practiced in a wider variety of settings, their title changed again to speech and language pathologists.

10. How does a developmental disorder differ from one that is acquired?

A developmental language delay means that a child is slow in developing adequate vocabulary and grammar or a language age that does not correspond to the child's chronological age. Acquire language delay can occur at any age and is the result of functional or organic etiologies. Early intervention has a positive impact on developmental language delays. It also has a positive impact on acquired delays if they occur early in the child's life.

11. How has family-centered early intervention influenced remediation strategies for young children with speech and language disorders?

Allowing parents to share concerns and participate equally in their child's education empowers them as partners in the habilitation process. It encourages involvement with the child and increases the effectiveness in treating communication disorders.

12. List an age-appropriate developmental milestone for a child two to three years of age.

Developmental milestones in language development for children two to three years of age include talks to other children as well as adults, solves problems by talking instead of hitting or crying, answer "where" questions, names common pictures and things, matches three to four colors, uses short sentences, knows basic concepts of size.

13. Define expressive and receptive language.

Receptive language is the ability to understand what is meant by spoken communication. Expressive language involves production of language that is understood by and meaningful to others.

14. Describe an effective informal measure of communications skills for the young child.

An effective informal measure of communication skills for young children is family-directed assessment. This focuses on family needs, concerns, and priorities. Families also help determine the type of support services needed by their children.

15. What difficulties are inherent to assessment of speech and language skills in a culturally diverse population?

Often tests used to assess language are based on European English. Assessments of other cultures frequently are biased because students are being judged by norms from a different population. Also differences in pragmatics and syntax are often the result of cultural variations. They do not represent linguistic delays. In assessing students from various cultures, differences should not be viewed as delays.

16. Define AAC, and describe its use by children with speech and language disorders.

These are symbols, aids, strategies, and techniques used to enhance the communication process. Augmentative or alternative communication can utilize electronic or non-electronic language boards. The item choices on the non-electronic language boards are real items, pictures of items, or symbols of items. The electronic language boards utilize voice as part of the communication system. Another augmentative or alternative communication example is frequency modulated systems. These systems help children who are hearing impaired to hear the speech of the teacher and filter out background noise.

CHAPTER TEN
PERSONS WITH HEARING IMPAIRMENTS

Overview of Persons with Hearing Impairments

This chapter examines the issues involved in the area of education for individuals with hearing impairments. The author examines definitions, possible causes, and educational alternatives in the field. Further, types of hearing impairments are discussed as well as the concepts of full educational inclusion and the Deaf culture.

Chapter Key Points

- Hearing impaired includes individuals who are deaf and those who are hard of hearing.
- Individuals who are deaf do not process linguistic information through audition.
- People who are hard of hearing can use hearing to process linguistic information.
- Conductive, sensorineural, mixed, and central hearing are the major types of hearing losses.
- Pure-tone audiometry is used to measure a person's hearing
- The Deaf culture feels individuals who are deaf feel more comfortable in their own culture with others who experience hearing problems.
- Oral, manual, and total communication are three main communication strategies used with individuals who are hearing impaired.
- Technology assists individuals with hearing impairments in meeting their full potential.
- Full inclusion may not be the least restrictive educational environment for children who are hearing impaired.

Focus and Reflect

1. Discuss the concept of a Deaf culture.

_____

_____

_____

2. Discuss the role of an audiologist.

_____

_____

_____

3. Does an inclusive classroom meet the needs of children with hearing impairments?

_____

_____

_____

4. Describe three uses of technology to meet the needs of children with hearing impairments.

_____

_____

_____

Chapter Guided Review

1. Definitions and concepts in the field of hearing impairment
   a. hearing impairment-general term used to describe disordered hearing
   b. hearing sensitivity loss-mild to profound
   c. deaf-hearing loss that is so severe that child is impaired in processing linguistic information through hearing
   d. hard of hearing-enough residual hearing to hear and understand speech
   e. anatomy of the auditory system-external ear, middle ear, inner ear, central auditory nervous system
   f. movement of sound-through external ear, ear canal, tympanic membrane, ossicles (malleus, incus, and stapes), oval window, cochlea, organ of Corti, auditory nervous system, and auditory cortex in the brain
   g. classification of hearing loss-conductive, sensori-neural, mixed, and functional hearing loss; central hearing disorder
   h. measurement of hearing loss-audiologist evaluates hearing; audiogram graphs hearing test results; pure tone audiometry used to test hearing (air-conduction and bond conduction are types of pure tone audiometry)
   i. other types of hearing assessment-case study, visual inspection of ear, pure-tone audiometry, measurement of speech recognition threshold, auditory evoked potentials (the brain's response to sound); evoke otoacoustic emissions (functions of inner ear); acoustic immittance (middle ear function)
   j. age of onset-prelingual hearing impairment (present before development of speech), postlingual hearing impairment (development of hearing impairment after development of speech)
2. A brief history of the field
   a. 1817-Gallaudet established American Asylum for Education of Deaf and Dumb in Hartford, Connecticut
   b. 1819-American School for the Deaf established in Massachusetts
   c. 1864-Gallaudet University established
   d. 1970s-total communication adopted (combined oral and manual communication approaches)
   e. 2000s-least restrict environment often means inclusive educational setting
3. Prevalence of hearing impairment
   a. 8.6% of the population of the United States has a hearing impairment
   b. prevalence of hearing impairment increases with age
4. Etiology of hearing impairment
   a. genetic/hereditary factors-autosomal dominant (ex., Waardenburg syndrome), autosomal recessive (ex. Usher's syndrome), and X-linked inheritance (ex. progressive sensori-neural hearing loss)
   b. infections-rubella, cytomegalovirus, hepatitis B virus, syphilis, measles, mumps, bacterial meningitis, and otitis media
   c. developmental abnormalities - atresia (malformation of the external or middle ear)
   d. environmental/traumatic factors-antibiotics, low birthweight, asphyxia, intense noise, head injuries, dramatic pressure changes in the middle ear
5. Characteristics of persons with hearing impairments
   a. intelligence-a function of language development
   b. speech and language-language delays minimized by early diagnosis of hearing impairment; often display significant articulation, voice quality and tone discrimination problems
   c. social development-less language interaction during play, less cooperative peer play, lack of language hinders overall social-emotional growth
   d. educational achievement-often three to four years below age appropriate grade levels, median reading level of third grade for sixteen and eighteen year old students with hearing impairments
6. Assessment of individuals with hearing impairment

a. cognitive assessment-Wechsler Intelligence Scale for Children-3rd edition; Hiskey-Nebraska Test of Learning Aptitude; Stanford Achievement Test (SAT)
b. communication assessment-stresses form of language, content of language, and use of language
c. person/social behavioral assessments-evaluates social adjustment, self-image, and emotional adjustment

7. Educational considerations
    a. Where are students with hearing impairments served?-regular public school programs and special school programs; influencing factors include degree of loss, age of onset, mode of communication, presence of other disabilities, and available resources; eighty percent of children with hearing impairments attend public school
    b. public school programs-programs include inclusive classroom settings, resource rooms, self-contained classrooms, and itinerant services
    c. special school programs-goals: positive learning environment, sense of belonging, personal identification, acceptance of hearing impairment; dramatic decline in enrollment since the mid-1970s
    d. instructional interventions-sign language, oral communication, auditory-verbal, cued speech, total communication, and Rochester Method (finger spelling); auditory-oral approach, total communication, bilingual-bicultural approach; most public schools use total communication; residential programs use bilingual-bicultural approach; related services provided by audiologist, interpreters, oral interpreters

8. Services for young children with hearing impairments
    a. newborn screening for hearing impairments
    b. early intervention-language information, communication skills; training in amplification, self-help, and social-emotional development
    c. focus on helping child with hearing impairment within the structure of the family

9. Transition and individuals with hearing impairments
    a. transition planning-initiated at age fourteen
    b. support from universities mandated by Section 504 of the Rehabilitation Act of 1973
    c. six federally funded post-secondary programs for deaf and hard of hearing
    d. training for post-secondary experiences in areas of personal, social, and community adjustments

10. Services for adults with hearing impairments
    a. State Commission on Deafness-services: advocacy, information, referral to agencies, interpreting services, job placement
    b. vocational rehabilitation services-vocational evaluation, job placement, counseling. Help in development of transition plan
    c. National Association for the Deaf-advocacy for deaf population at state and federal levels
    d. Alexander Graham Bell Association-materials and technology related to oral teaching methods

11. Family issues
    a. family reaction-shock, disbelief, grief, frustration, denial, depression, anxiety, blame spouse, overprotective of child, acceptance of hearing impairment, use of parent support groups
    b. siblings and grandparents-close relationships with sibling who is hearing impaired, resentment reaction; grandparents concerned about own child and grandchild
    c. issues of diversity-forty percent of students with hearing impairments from culturally diverse populations; Deaf culture: own language, traditions, values, and literature

12. Technology and persons with hearing impairments
    a. hearing aids and auditory training devices-in-ear aids, behind-the-ear aids, body aids, bone conduction aids; differential amplification of frequencies in hearing aids; use of auditory trainers and sound field systems in classrooms
    b. computers-focus on speech drill, auditory training, sign language instruction, speech reading, and supplemental reading and language instruction; synthesize speech from key board input and transcribe speech onto a display screen
    c. captioning-caption functions for television and videotapes

    d. telecommunication devices-telecommunication device for the deaf (TDD); amplified telephones

    e. cochlear implants-surgically implanted devices into inner ear to make sounds audible; best when implanted early; improves high-frequency hearing ability

13. Trends, issues, and controversies
    a. appropriate methodology for educating hearing impaired children-aspects: kind of language and form of communication impacted by severity of hearing loss
    b. transitioning from child-centered to family-centered intervention programs-issues: communication methods, Deaf culture issues, appropriate standards and procedures for early intervention programs
    c. inclusion of hearing impaired children in regular education programs-issues: classroom teachers not familiar with the dynamics of deafness, not skilled in communication techniques, and students often stigmatized and isolated
    d. limited interaction between the Deaf culture and the hearing word-Deaf culture: deafness is nonpathelogical but its own culture.

Application Exercises & Project Suggestions

1. Interview an adult who is deaf. Report on his/her feelings concerning the concept of the Deaf culture.
2. Observe a preschool class for children with hearing impairments. What types of communication strategies were used to promote the development of language.
3. Discuss the capabilities of a hearing aid with an individual who uses one. Find out how his/her hearing aid has changed in its capabilities over time.

InfoTrac® Activity Suggestions

Activity 10.1: Prelingual deafness
This article discusses the challenges faced by children who are prelingually deaf.

1. Locate and read **"Implications of Prelingual Deafness"** by Cassia Margolis in **Lancet**.

2. Do prelingually deaf children ever develop good speech and speech reception skills?

_____

_____

3. Why do you think most children who are deaf and raised using oral communication eventually use sign language as adults?

_____

_____

_____

4. Can individuals who are deaf and have never heard language be fluent in English?

_____

_____

Activity 10.2: Hearing aids
This article discusses recent advancements in the development of hearing aids.

1. Locate and read **"Living with Hearing Loss"** by David Myers in the *Saturday Evening Post*.

2. Describe two advantages of digital aids.

_____

_____

_____

3. Discuss two types of hearing aids and the function of each.

_____

_____

_____

4. Discuss three signs of hearing loss.

_____

_____

_____

InfoTrac® Article Suggestions

- Nighswonger, T. (2001). The quest for hearing health. <u>Occupational Hazards, 63</u>, 64-73.
- Margolis, A. (2001). Implications of prelingual deafness. <u>The Lancet, 358</u>, 76.

Key Terms

Define each:

hearing impairment_____

hearing sensitivity loss_____

deaf_____

residual hearing_____

hard of hearing_____

external or outer ear_____

middle ear_____

inner ear_____

central auditory nervous system_____

tympanic membrane_____

malleus_____

incus_____

stapes_____

ossicular chain_____

oval window_____

cochlea_____

organ of Corti_____

conductive hearing loss_____

otitis media_____

sensorineural hearing loss_____

mixed hearing loss_____

central hearing loss_____

functional or nonorganic hearing loss_____

audiometric test_____

audiologist_____

audiogram_____

frequency_____

hertz (Hz)_____

decibels (dB)_____

pure-tone audiometry_____

air-conduction audiometry_____

bone-conduction audiometry_____

play audiometry_____

speech audiometry_____

speech recognition threshold (SRT)_____

auditory evoked potentials_____

evoked otoacoustic emissions_____

acoustic immittance_____

prelingual_____

postlingual_____

manual communcation_____

oral approaches_____

total communcation_____

adventitious (acquired) hearing loss_____

autosomal dominant_____

autosomal recessive_____

X-linked_____

atresia_____

fingerspelling_____

interpreter_____

oral interpreter_____

transliteration_____

high-risk register_____

assertive listening devices_____

auditory trainers_____

FM systems_____

signal-to-noise ratio_____

sound field systems_____

telecommunication device for the deaf (TDD)_____

amplified telephones_____

CHAPTER TEN: PERSONS WITH HEARING IMPAIRMENTS
Practice Test

True or False
1. The outer ear contains the malleus._____

2. The organ of Corti consists of 20,000 tiny hair cells located in the

cochlea._____

3. A sensori-neural hearing loss is caused by disorders of the inner ear and/or the auditory nerve

that transmits impulses to the brain._____

4. An audiologist is a physician who performs surgery on the ear._____

5. Hertz is a measurement of loudness of sound._____

6. Decibel is a measurement of the frequency of sound._____

7. Pure-tone audiometry uses air-conduction audiometry and bone-conduction

audiometry._____

8. Congenital hearing loss is present at birth._____

Multiple Choice

1. Autosomal dominant inheritance:
    a. is carried on one chromosome of a pair.
    b. must be carried by both genes of a pair to be expressed.
    c. is expressed as Waardenburg syndrome.
    d. none of the above.

2. Usher's syndrome is :
    a. caused by rubella
    b. caused by a bilateral hearing loss and retinitis pigmentosa
    c. is autosomal dominant
    d. all of the above.

3. Cytomegalovirus is :
    a. the most common viral infection causing hearing loss.
    b. contracted from the mother to the infant.
    c. progresses rapidly in the first year.
    d. all of the above.

4. Children with postlingual deafness:
    a. generally develop better speech, language, reading, and writing skills than prelingually deaf children.
    b. develop poorer language and academic skills than prelingually deaf children.
    c. must be identified as early as possible to initiate intervention.
    d. all of the above.

5. Manual communication stresses:
    a. verbal communication with the hearing world.
    b. signing
    c. attempt to prevent social isolation among individuals with hearing impairments.
    d. all of the above.

6. Today, the most widely used approach in public school programs for children who are hearing impaired is:
   a. oral communication
   b. manual communication
   c. total communication
   d. none of the above.

7. The nation's first university for the hearing impaired is:
   a. Notre Dame
   b. American School for the Deaf
   c. Gallaudet University
   d. Laurent Clerc National Deaf Education Center

8. Atresia is characterized by:
   a. lack or malformation of the outer ear.
   b. lack or malformation of the middle ear
   c. lack or malformation of the inner ear.
   d. none of the above.

9. Alexander Graham Bell favored:
   a. manual communication.
   b. oral communication.
   c. total communication.
   d. none of the above.

10. Individuals who are hearing impaired are frequently significantly behind in:
    a. motor skills.
    b. social skills.
    c. math skills.
    d. reading skills.

Matching

1. Deaf culture
2. hearing aids
3. public school programs
4. total communication
5. Gallaudet University
6. fingerspelling
7. cochlear implants
8. telecommunication device for the deaf (TDD)
9. adventitiously deaf
10. pure tone audiometry

a. educational placement of most children with hearing impairments.
b. a form of sign language using the manual alphabet
c. surgery to help sensori-neural hearing loss
d. believes that American Sign Language is the first language of people with hearing impairments.
e. measures sound recognition thresholds at various frequencies using increasing volume
f. born with normal hearing but sense of hearing has become non-functional because of illness or accident
g. first federally funded university
h. a small keyboard with an electronic display screen and modem
i. amplification aids which can selectively increase the volume of sounds at specific frequencies
j. uses a combination of oral and manual communication

Chapter 10: Persons with Hearing Impairments
Practice Test Answer Key

True or False
1. False. The outer ear is made up of the pinna and the auditory canal.
2. True
3. True
4. False. An audiologist provides evaluation, rehabilitation, and prevention services to individuals with hearing impairments.
5. False. Hertz is a measurement of the frequency of sound.
6. False. Decibel is a measurement of the loudness of sound.
7. True
8. True

Multiple Choice
1. A and C
2. B
3. D
4. A and C
5. B and C
6. C
7. C
8. A
9. B
10. C and D

Matching
1. D
2. I
3. A
4. J
5. G
6. B
7. C
8. H
9. F
10. E

Check Your Understanding ⇨ See textbook page 446
Answer Key

1. Define the terms deaf and hard of hearing.
Hard of hearing describes individuals who have enough residual hearing to hear and understand speech. Deaf is used to describe individuals for whom the sense of hearing is non-functional for the ordinary purposes of life. The person is impaired in processing linguistic information through hearing, with or without, amplification.

2. Why is it important to know the age of onset, type, and degree of hearing loss?
Age of onset of hearing loss is critical because normal language development depends on an intact auditory system. The severity of speech communication disorders is directly related to the degree or severity of hearing loss. Knowing the type of hearing loss is critical in intervention strategies. Conductive losses often can be helped through surgical interventions and amplification systems. Sensori-neural losses can not be helped through surgery. An exceptional to this is cochlear implantation.

3. What is the primary difference between prelingual and postlingual hearing impairment?
Prelingual hearing impairment is disordered hearing present at birth or occurring before the development of speech and language. Post lingual hearing impairment describes an auditory deficit acquired after the acquisition of speech and language.

4. List the four major types of hearing loss.
The four major types of hearing loss are conductive hearing loss where sound is not conducted normally through mechanical sound-conducting mechanisms. Sensori-neural hearing loss is caused by disorders of the inner ear and/or the auditory nerve that transmits impulses to the brain. Mixed hearing loss is a combination of both conductive and sensorineural loss. Central hearing disorder is a dysfunction in the central auditory nervous system between the brain stem and auditory cortex in the brain.

5. Describe three different types of audiological evaluations.
Pure-tone audiometry is the basic hearing evaluation. It measures hearing thresholds in terms of loudness (decibels) needed to recognize the presence of a sound a various frequencies (hertz). Pure-tone audiometry uses the modes of air-conduction audiometry and bone-conduction audiometry. A second type of audiometry is play audiometry for children difficult to test or unable to follow commands. A third type of evaluation is speech audiometry that measures an individual's recognition of speech in various listening conditions.

6. What are some major areas of development that are usually affected by a hearing impairment?
Some major areas of development that are affected by hearing impairment are speech, language, reading, and writing skills. Hearing impairments also effect social/cognitive development and academic achievement.

7. List three major causes of hearing impairment.
Three major causes of hearing impairment are autosomal dominant inheritance conditions (ex. Waardenburg syndrome), autosomal recessive inheritance conditions (ex. Usher's syndrome), and X-linked inheritance (ex. autosomal recessive early-onset progressive sensori-neural hearing loss). Also infections, developmental abnormalities and environmental factors cause hearing impairments.

8. What issues are central to the manualism versus oralism debate.

The manual approach believes that children with hearing impairments can learn when expectations are high, should not feel isolated from society, can participate in general life activities, and can benefit socially by having friends with common interests. The oral position in educating children with hearing impairments believes that the manual approach fosters segregation of individuals from mainstream society. The oral approach stresses integration into a society that uses oral language. In the past, the oral approach has been more widely accepted than the manual approach in educating children with hearing impairments.

9. Define the concept of a Deaf culture.

The Deaf culture considers a hearing impairment to be non-pathelogical. This culture opposes medical interventions to improve hearing impairments. Individuals with hearing impairments often work in a hearing world but have family and social lives in a deaf world. Proponents of the Deaf culture believe individuals with hearing impairments would prefer to spend their lives in their own culture.

10. What is total communication, and how can it be used in the classroom?

Total communication is a combination of manual and oral communication. Total communication stresses the concept of whatever works best for each child. It uses a variety of singing systems. Total communication in the classroom is based on the idea that simultaneous use of various communication strategies enhances an individual's ability to communicate, comprehend, and learn.

11. Describe the bilingual-bicultural approach to educating pupils with hearing impairments.

The bilingual-bicultural approach considers American Sign Language to be the natural language of the Deaf   American Sign Language. In addition, English instruction stresses vocabulary and syntax rules.

12. In what two academic areas do students with hearing impairments usually lag behind their classmates?

Hearing impaired students are behind their hearing peers in the academic areas of reading and math. The median performance levels in reading and math were third and seventh grade respectively for students with hearing impairments.

13. Why is early identification of a hearing impairment important?

Early intervention is critical in the development of expressive and receptive communication skills. Not identifying hearing loss has a profoundly negative impact on the development of language, speech, and educational achievement. Early intervention programs provide families information on language development, communication skills, amplification systems, self-help, and social-emotional development for children.

14. Why do professionals assess the language and speech abilities of individuals with hearing impairments?

Language and speech abilities of individuals with hearing impairments are assessed to determine the impact of hearing impairments. A mild to moderate hearing impairment may result in minimal effects in the development of language. Prelingual moderate hearing impairments result in the ability to hear only voiced sounds. This loss can be helped with treatment and technology. Children who are deaf exhibit articulation problems, voice quality, and tone discrimination problems.

15. List five indicators of a possible hearing loss in the classroom.

Five indicators of children having hearing loss are hearing difficulty in a noisy classroom setting, difficulty distinguishing distant sounds, significant delays in speech and language, reduced vocabulary, articulation deficits, poor voice quality, and difficulty mastering grammatical and syntactical concepts.

16. What are three indicators in children that may predict success with a cochlear implant?

Indicators in children that predict success using a cochlear implant include early cochlear implants (before age six), degree of hearing loss, age of onset of hearing loss, family support, previous experience with amplification, and supportive educational methodology.

17. Identify five strategies a classroom teacher can use to promote communicative skills and enhance independence in the transition to adulthood.

A classroom teacher can facilitate the transition to adulthood through the development of a transition plan in collaboration with the student with a hearing impairment and his/her family. Further, the teacher can gather information with other professionals to make educational placements and communicate training decisions. Also the teacher can provide information to parents concerning legislation mandating accessibility at colleges and universities for individuals with disabilities as well as assist in transitions into new educational and vocational environments. Finally, teacher can provide assistance in the area of career counseling.

18. Describe how to check a hearing aid.

The teacher can check a hearing aid by using a stethoscope to check the quality of sound provided by the hearing aid. Also the teacher can use a battery checker to check the batteries in a hearing aid. Other checks should include hearing aid functions (sound cuts on and off, voice distorted), student's functioning ability with the hearing aid(response to sounds at predetermined distances), and general hearing aid problems (hearing aid on, good battery, dirt or wax in ear mold).

19. How can technology benefit individuals with a hearing impairment?

Technology can be used to enhance a person with a hearing impairment's integration into the hearing world. Hearing aids now allow differential amplification at different frequencies that match the needs of the user. Also auditory trainers and sound field systems can be used in the classroom to amplify sound and reduce noise for children. Computers are used for speech drill, auditory training, sign language instruction, speech reading, supplemental reading, and language instruction. Other technology includes alerting devices, closed captions of television programs and videotapes, telecommunication devices for the deaf (TDD), and amplified telephones.

CHAPTER ELEVEN
PERSONS WITH VISUAL IMPAIRMENTS

Overview of Visual Impairments

The goal of this chapter is to provide an understanding of the visual process, vision loss, and the effects of visual loss on vocational skills and school performance. The authors have studied historical foundations of the field of visual impairments, types of visual loss, educational practices, and technological interventions to assist the reader in adapting the general educational curriculum for students with visual impairments.

Chapter Key Points

- Visual impairment includes blindness and low vision.
- The eye is composed of various structures which allow us to transmit images to the brain and in turn see our surroundings.
- There are a number of conditions which result in visual loss for children. These include cataracts, glaucoma, problems with the optic nerve, myopia, hyperopia, and astigmatism as well as retinopathy of prematurity.
- Screening for visual problems are often conducted at school using a Snellen Chart. Children found to have visual problems are referred to ophthalmologist or optometrists.
- A team approach involving the child, his/her family, and various educational and medical specialists is used in developing appropriate educational and mobility services for the student with visual impairments.

Focus and Reflect

Discuss three accommodation needs of children with visual impairments.

_____

_____

_____

Discuss the major components of the anatomy of the eye.

_____

_____

Discuss the impact of visual loss of a child on the family.

_____

_____

Discuss the concept of literacy mediums for individuals with visual impairments.

_____

_____

Chapter Guided Review

1. Visual impairment: Impairment in vision that even with correction adversely affects an individual's educational performance.

2. Visual acuity: Clarity of vision

3. Visual accommodation: The ability of the eye to see up close and at a distance.

4. Legal blindness: 20/200 in the best eye after corrections or a visual field no greater than 20 degrees.

5. Blind: Uses tactual and auditory as primary channels of learning.

6. Low vision: A person with low vision uses residual vision with the help of lighting and magnification to see up close.

7. Deaf-blind: Children who have severe impairments in both vision and hearing. A child does not have to be totally deaf and totally blind to be classified as deaf-blind.

8. Anatomy of the eye from front to back: Cornea, iris (with pupil in the center of the iris), aqueous humor, lens, vitreous humor, retina (macula is in the central part of the retina), optic nerve, brain. Vision occurs in the brain not in the eye.

9. Conditions resulting in visual impairments:
   a. hyperopia
   b. myopia
   c. astigmatism
   d. cataracts
   e. glaucoma
   f. optic nerve atrophy
   g. albinism
   h. eye injury
   i. ROP (Retinopathy or Prematurity)
   j. Amblyopia (Lazy eye)- a severe form of strabismus
   k. Nystagmus
   l. Photophobia
   m. Macula degeneration
   n. Retinitis pigmentosa
   o. Coloboma

10. History
    a. Louis Braille
    b. Perkins School for the Blind
    c. Sight saving schools
    d. The concept of visual efficiency-Barraga

11. Behavioral characteristics of children with visual impairments
    a. watery eyes
    b. turning of head, body, or eyes
    c. uses markers when reading
    d. poor grades
    e. difficulty with color identification
    f. misaligns math columns
    g. confusion in writing numbers and letters
    h. requires additional time to do a task
    i. fails to make eye contact when talking to people

12. Social and emotional development
    a. Low vision child will pair visual and tactual experiences in social situations
    b. Children who are legally blind retrieve information tactually and auditorially
    c. Blind children use tactual and auditory clues in the environment. They may use their hands to describe objects
    d. Vocational skill training stresses functional life skills, self-help, and independence skills at and early age

13. Assessment of students with visual impairments
    a. Most schools use a Snellen chart to identify children with visual problems
    b. Students identified as having visual problems are referred to the optometrist or opthamologist
    c. A vision exam frequently consists of acuity test, visual field tests, and interview with student.
    d. A functional vision assessment uses vision in a variety of environments as well as the development of intervention suggestions.
    e. A learning media assessment consists of determining a student's preferred method of reading and writing and considers regular size print, large print, and braille.
    f. Educational assessment focuses on academic skills, learning media, communication skills, social interaction skills, orientation and mobility skills, independent living skills, vocational skills, assistive technology, and visual efficiency.

14. Instructional considerations
    a. Curricular concerns focus on academic skills, sensory perception, orientation and mobility, social living skills, daily living skills, communication, vocational skills, self-help skills, recreation and leisure, and transition skills.
    b. Supportive services include adaptive technology, transcription services, resources for equipment, activities of daily living, communication education, and orientation and mobility, and reader services.

15. Age level needs of children with visual impairments
    a. Programs for young children often focus on sensory development, gross motor development, fine motor development, socialization, language development, and self-help skills. These skills are reflected on the child's IEP or IFSP.
    b. Transition to adulthood programs focus on vocational selection, developing transition plans, travel skills, low vision devices, reading materials, family education, and an awareness of resources in the community.
    c. Adult programs focus on transportation, low vision evaluations, social opportunities, technology support, and orientation and mobility.

16. Technology needs
    a. Children often need to be evaluated for their specific needs.
    b. APH and AFB provide services and support in the area of technology
    c. Technology plays a critical role in current software and hardware for the population with visual impairments.

17. Trends
    a. Teacher shortage in the special education of visual impairments
    b. There is a shortage of orientation and mobility specialists.
    c. Case loads for specialists in visual impairments are large.
    d. A team approach is frequently used in determining services for children with visual impairments.
    e. There are not enough appropriate materials to use in the assessment of children with visual impairments.
    f. Transition issues focus on independence of children, vocational preparation, and support of families and community services.

Application Exercises & Project Suggestions

1. Eat while wearing a blindfold. What were the most difficult aspects of this experience? Did it seem to be disorienting? Did the food taste the same to you? Did you feel self-conscious?
2. Observe a model of the eye. Trace the path of light through the eye from the cornea to the optic nerve. Identify specific parts of the eye as you are following the path of light.
3. Interview an optometrist or an opthamologist. Discuss what evaluations these professionals might use when he/she evaluates the vision of an individual with visual impairments.
4. Describe what the color blue means to a person who has been blind from birth? How would you try to teach this concept to a child with congenital blindness?

InfoTrac® Activity Suggestions

Activity 1.1: Diabetes I
This activity is based on an article, which reviews the impact of diabetes on vision. The article provides intervention strategies.

1. Locate and read "**Save Your Sight : Loss Of Vision Is One Of The Most Feared Complications Of Diabetes.**" This article is written by Gerald Rogell and appeared in the December 2001 issue of *Diabetes Forecast*.

2. What are the three major causes of severe vision loss from diabetes?

_____

_____

_____

3. Discuss the role of eye exams in preventing or lessening the effects of diabetic retinopathy.

_____

_____

_____

Activity 1.2 Vision screening
This activity is based on an article that reviews suggested guidelines for vision screening in infants, children, and young adults.
1. Locate and read "AAP Issues Guidelines For Vision Screening In Infants, Children And Young Adults". This article appeared in the December 1997 issue of *American Family Physician*.

2. Name four components of an eye examination.

_____

_____

_____

3. Name three screening tests which can be used with children.

_____

_____

_____

InfoTrac® Article Suggestions
- Katz, H. (2000). Walk a mile with my eyes. <u>Maclean's</u>, <u>1</u>, 9.
- Granet, D. (1999). Vision screening. <u>The Exceptional Parent</u>, <u>29</u>, 180.

Key Terms
Define each:

visually impaired _____

visual field_____

field loss_____

fixation_____

legally blind_____

Snellen chart_____

functionally blind_____

primary literacy medium_____

low vision_____

residual vision_____

deaf-blind_____

cornea_____

iris_____

pupil_____

lens_____

vitreous humor_____

retina_____

macula_____

optic nerve_____

myopia_____

hyperopia_____

astigmatism_____

orbit_____

cataracts_____

glaucoma_____

optic nerve _____

atrophy_____

albinism_____

retinopathy of prematurity_____

braille_____

visual efficiency_____

photophobic_____

aphakic_____

rods_____

cells_____

macular degeneration_____

retinitis pigmentosa_____

coloboma_____

visual screening_____

functional vision_____

literacy medium_____

learning media_____

grade 1 braille_____

grade 2 braille _____

orientation and mobility_____

CHAPTER ELEVEN: PERSONS WITH VISUAL IMPAIRMENTS
Practice Test

True or False
1. Vision occurs in the eye. _____

2. ROP is caused by a lack of oxygen. _____

3. The crystal-like portion of the eye is called the lens. _____

4. Low vision students utilize magnification aids to assist with near vision. _____

5. A coloboma is a keyhole appearing opening in the iris. _____

6. Glaucoma is a condition, which occurs in individuals over thirty years of age. _____

7. Rods are cells in the retina which are color sensitive. _____

8. Adults with visual impairments need assistance in learning to be self-sufficient. _____

9. Retinitis pigmentosa is a visual condition existing from birth. _____

Multiple Choice
1. A physician who performs surgery on the eye is an _____
   a. ophthalmologist
   b. optician
   c. optometrist
   d. orthopedist

2. A specialist who trains individuals with visual impairments in the area of mobility is a
   _____.
   a. optician
   b. low vision specialist
   c. orientation and mobility specialist
   d. none of the above

3. The type of braille that is most frequently used is _____.
   a. grade 1
   b. grade 2
   c. grade 3
   d. none of the above

4. The central part of the retina where an image comes to focus is called the _____.
   a. macula
   b. aqueous humor
   c. lens
   d. cornea

5. An eye condition which is characterized by increased pressure in the eye is called
   _____.
   a. cataracts
   b. glaucoma
   c. retinitis pigmentosa
   d. macular degeneration

6. Two modifications which can be used in the assessment of children with visual impairments
   may include _____ and _____.
   a. additional time
   b. large print
   c. larger classroom
   d. speaking louder

7. Two problems which may be faced by adults with visual impairments are _____ and
   _____.
   a. long term residential placement
   b. orientation and mobility
   c. depression
   d. no social skills

Matching

Retinitis pigmentosa	Lens
Visual acuity	Astigmatism
Orientation	Glaucoma
Snellen chart	Retinopathy of prematurity
Iris	Grade one braille

1. _____refers to the ability to visually perceive details.

2. _____ where each letter of a word is spelled out with the Braille letter corresponding to the print letter.

3. _____being aware of where you are, where you are going, and the route to get there.

4. _____ is a clinical measurement of the true amount of distance vision an individual has under certain conditions.

5. _____is one or more surfaces of the cornea or lens that are not spherical but are cylindrical.

6. _____ is the transparent disc in the middle of the eye behind the pupil that brings rays of light into focus on the retina.

7. _____ is the colored, circular part of the eye in front of the lens.

8. _____ occurs when the vascular growth has been interrupted due to premature birth.

9. _____is the major disease that occurs in the aqueous.

10. _____is a hereditary condition resulting in the gradual degeneration of the retina.

Chapter 11: Visual Impairments
Practice Test Answer Key

True or False
1. False. Vision occurs in the brain.
2. False. ROP is caused by too much oxygen.
3. True
4. False. Low vision students use magnification to assist with near and distant vision.
5. True
6. False. Glaucoma is a condition which can occur at any age.
7. False. Rods are cells in the retina of the eye which are sensitive to black and white and assist in night vision.
8. True
9. True

Multiple Choice
1. A.
2. C.
3. B.
4. A.
5. B
6. A.
7. B.

Matching
1. visual acuity
2. grade 1 braille
3. orientation
4. Snellen chart
5. astigmatism
6. lens
7. iris
8. retinopathy of prematurity
9. glaucoma
10. retinitis pigmentosa

Check Your Understanding ⇨ **See textbook page 486**
Answer Key

1. **What is the legal definition of blindness? How does it differ from the IDEA definition?**
The IDEA definition of visual impairment is vision that even with correction adversely affects an individual's educational performance. Legally blind is 20/200 in the better eye with correction or a visual field no greater than 20 degrees.

2. **What does the Snellen chart assess? What does 20/200 mean?**
The Snellen chart measures the true amount of distance vision a person has under certain conditions. The acuity measurement of 20/200 means that 20 feet is the distance at which visual acuity is measured and 200 feet is the distance a person with normal vision would be able to identify the largest symbol on the eye chart.

3. **Describe how the eye functions?**
Light enters the eye through the cornea then through the pupil in the iris. Light progresses through the aqueous humor and is brought to a focus by the crystalline lens. The light moves through the vitreous humor and is focused on the central part of the retina called the macula. The retina changes light into electrical impulses and the electrical impulses are sent along the optic nerve to the brain. Vision takes place in the brain not in the eye.

4. **Define the terms myopia, hyperopia, and astigmatism.**
In myopia, incoming light focuses in front of the retina (called nearsightedness). In hyperopia, incoming light has not come to a focus when it reaches the retina (called farsightedness).

5. **List five eye problems in school age children.**
   a. cataracts
   b. glaucoma
   c. optic nerve atrophy
   d. myopia
   e. eye injury

6. **Why is early detection important in the detection of vision problems?**
Early screening and diagnosis can detect the prognosis of visual impairments. Screenings and eye exams should start after birth, at six months, before entering school, and throughout the school years.

7. **Describe social and emotional characteristics of persons with visual impairments.**
Many individuals with visual impairments do not respond visually to people in the environment. People with visual impairments may be left out of social events. Individuals may actually talk for people with visual impairments. Individuals with visual impairments may feel isolated and have low self-esteem.

8. **What is functional vision and how is it evaluated?**
Functional vision is how well a student uses his/her vision to complete a specific task and is evaluated by observing the student in a variety of settings and activities. It should consider near and distant visual abilities. Functional vision assessment should include an evaluation of the student's travel skills and samples of the student's work.

9. **Define the term learning media. Give three examples of different forms of learning media.**
Learning media includes the methods and materials a student uses in conjunction with the sensory channels to learn. Three examples of learning media are visual learning media, tactual learning, and auditory learning media.

10. **In what two educational settings do the majority of students with a visual impairment receive a special education?**
Most students with visual impairments receive special education services in the general education classroom and in the resource room setting.

11. **What are some of the common educational accommodations that a student with visual impairments might require?**
Some of the more common educational accommodations are in the areas of academics, leisure time activities, and daily living/self-help activities. Academic modifications include closed circuit television, videotapes, word processing programs, talking clocks, and speech output devices. Leisure time activity modifications include adapted games, buzzers, lifts for swimming pools, and descriptive videos. Daily living adaptations include braille labels, large print telephone buttons, magnifiers, and lifts for automobiles and chairs.

12. **List five signs of possible vision problems in children.**
    a. watery eyes
    b. eye fatigue
    c. frequent headaches
    d. poor grades
    e. requires additional time to complete tasks

13. **Identify three critical issues which must be addressed if an adolescent is to successfully transition to post-secondary education or enter the workforce.**
Three major issues for adolescents with visual impairments include vocational selection, use of low vision devices, community resources, and independence on the job.

14. **Besides cultural differences, what diversity issue must be addressed for parents who are also visually impaired?**
Parents who are visually impaired face the diversity issue of requiring the use of braille or large print for written documents.

15. **Identify five technology accommodations that can be provided for a student who is legally blind in high school.**
Five technology accommodations for high school students who are legally blind include the use of computers, books on tape, speech output devices for computers, Versabraillers to convert print to braille and vice versa, and e-mail.

16. **Discuss the shortage of orientation and mobility specialists and how a child's performance is affected when there is a shortage of personnel.**
There is a lack of orientation and mobility specialists. This affects the number of hours available to fulfill the IEP goals of each child. With more personnel comes a reduction in case loads and a stable service delivery system for individuals with visual impairments.

CHAPTER TWELVE
PERSONS WITH AUTISM

Overview of Autism
The goal of this chapter is to provide an understanding of autism. The author has described a multiaxial system, which provides a more complete description of autism. The chapter provides a brief overview of a definition of autism, characteristics of the condition, and suggestions for education interventions. In addition, the effectiveness of various popular medical and language interventions in the area of autism are reviewed.

Chapter Key Points
- Autism is one of five disorders in pervasive developmental disorders.
- Autism has a spectrum of characteristics in terms of severity.
- The three main characteristics of autism are social interaction deficits, communication deficits, and the presence of repetitive and restricted interest. These conditions are present by age three.
- Autism may be associated with other conditions such as tuberous sclerosis, Fragile X, Tourette syndrome, William's syndrome, Angelman syndrome, and Down Syndrome.
- Effective intervention in autism includes classroom structure, language stimulation, early intervention, and involving families in the education process.

Focus and Reflect
1. Discuss the concept that bad parenting causes autism.

_____

_____

_____

2. Discuss three possible causative factors associated with autism. (Abnormalities of the brain, autoimmune factors, chromosomal/ genetic factors.)

_____

_____

_____

3. Discuss applied behavioral analysis as it applies to children with autism.

_____

_____

_____

4. Discuss three living alternatives for adults with autism. (Residential care, group home, adult foster care.)

_____

_____

_____

Chapter Guided Review

1. Autism - A complex developmental disability that appears during the first three years of life and results in difficulties in verbal and non-verbal communications, social interactions, and leisure/play activities.

2. Kanner coined the term autism, meaning escape from reality.

3. Autism differs from schizophrenia in the areas of extreme aloneness from the beginning of life, attachment to objects, powerful desire for sameness.

4. Autism is a complex medical disorder with genetic, environmental, and neurological causes.

5. The DSM-IV-TR by the American Psychiatric Association and Individuals with Disabilities, with Disabilities Education Act, 1997 provide diagnostic systems used to diagnose and classify autism.

6. Autism is a pervasive developmental disorder that is often referred to as a spectrum disorder.

7. Conditions included in the diagnostic category of pervasive developmental disorder with Autism: Rett's disorder, childhood disintegrative disorder Asperger's disorder, and not-otherwise specified pervasive developmental disorder.

8. Classification systems in autism:
    a. Mild, moderate, severe depending on level of mental retardation.
    b. Autistic savant- ten percent of autistic population has skills in math, memory, artistic, and musical and reading abilities.
    c. Hyperlexia - Ability to read by age two to five but without understanding of what they read. (one percent of individuals with autism.)

9. Medical Conditions Associated with autism.
    a. tuberous sclerosis
    b. Fragile X syndrome
    c. Gilles de la Tourette syndrome
    d. Angelman syndrome
    e. Landau-Kleffner syndrome
    f. William's syndrome
    g. Down's Syndrome

10. History of autism.
    a. autism initially blamed on bad mothering (psychogenic theories concerning the cause of autism) - Bettleheim
    b. Rimland - advocated a biological base for autism
    c. Bender - felt autism was biologically based
    d. Fester, Lovaas - advocated applied behavioral analysis as a method of helping children with autism

11. Prevalence of autism
    a. ranges from two to five cases per 10,000 to one in five hundred cases.
    b. Incidence of autism on rise
        i. clinicians evaluating more accurately
        ii. more babies are surviving
        iii. special education legislation has mandated early intervention and specialized services
        iv. different diagnostic criteria are being used to identify autism today

12. Etiology of autism
    a. Genetic and Chromosomal Factors
        i.   25% of autism associated with genetic factors
        ii.   5-10% of autism due to medical disorders
    b. Insults during Pregnancy
        i.   lack of oxygen at birth
        ii.   thalidomide
        iii.   congenital rubella
        iv.   measles
        v.   mumps
        vi.   encephalitis
        vii.   birth order
        viii.   abnormal CNS function
    c. Abnormalities of the Brain
        i.   altered role of neurotransmitters
        ii.   dysfunctions of brain systems
    d. Autoimmune and Environmental Factors
        i.   food allergies – milk, wheat,
        ii.   vitamin deficiencies – B6 and magnesium may help improve metabolism

13. Characteristics of People with Autism
    a. quantitative impairment in social interaction (2 symptoms must be present in this category for identification)
        i.   fails to develop age appropriate peer relationships
        ii.   lack of ability to share interests and achievements of others
        iii.   lacks social and emotional reciprocity
        iv.   lacks coordinated gaze
    b. impairment in communication (1 symptom must be present in the category for identification)
        i.   delay of lack of spoken language
        ii.   marked impairment in conversation skills
        iii.   stereotypic use of language (echolalia)
        iv.   lack of spontaneous make-believe or social play
        v.   speech is literal in meaning
        vi.   reversal of pronouns
        vii.   abnormal rhythm pitch of speech
    c. restrictive, repetitive and stereotyped patterns of behavior (1 symptom must be present in this category for identification)
        i.   preoccupation with at least 1 stereotyped pattern of interest
        ii.   inflexible adherence to non-functional rituals
        iii.   stereotypic motor mannerisms
        iv.   preoccupation with parts of objects
        v.   obsessions – time consuming and interfere with normal routine
    d. concentration problems
        i.   hyperactivity
        ii.   impulsivity
        iii.   short attention
    e. self-injurious behavior
    f. abnormalities in eating
    g. sleeping problems
    h. abnormalities of mood and affect
        i.   depression
        ii.   suicidal at times
        iii.   swings in mood for no apparent reason
        iv.   absence of emotion reaction
    i. sensory Impairment

     i.   high threshold of pain
     ii.   tactual defensiveness
     iii.   exaggerated response to light and sound

14. Assessment of Autism
    a. Splinter skills exist in some individuals with autism.
    b. 50-70 % of people with autism have mental retardation
    c. decreases in cognitive and adaptive functioning in adolescence
    d. rating scales
       i.   Childhood Autism Rating Scale
       ii.   Autistic Screening Instrument for Educational Planning
       iii.   Autism Behavior Checklist
    e. behavioral assessments
    f. functional assessments

15. Educational Considerations
    a. Predictable educational environment
    b. Most children with autism educated in self-contained classes
    c. Early intervention
       i.   may result in higher IQ, more speech, reduced behavior problems
       ii.   utilizes parent counseling, assistive technology, occupational therapy, etc.
       iii.   Lovaas-intensive early behavioral intervention in all of the child's environments by all significant people
    d. Transition services
       i.   Planning for transition starts at age 14
       ii.   includes individual, family, and community agencies
       iii.   involves daily living, exposure to community experiences, development of employment objectives, and functional vocational evaluation

16. Services for Adults with Autism
    a. 1/3 of adults with autism achieve some degree of independence
    b. residential care
       i.   group homes
       ii.   supervised apartment living
       iii.   adult foster care
    c. employment options
       i.   sheltered workshops
       ii.   job coach

17. Family issues
    a. presence of child with autism stressful for family
    b. diagnosis of condition may help families
    c. siblings often help with demands of children with autism

18. Technology
    a. computers
    b. voice output communication aids
    c. visual strategies (Picture Exchange Communication System)
    d. manual sign language

19. Trends, Issues, and Controversies
    a. sensory integration
    b. pharmacology
    c. vitamins
    d. food allergies
    e. auditory integration training

    f. facilitated communication
    g. secretin
    h. music therapy
    i. visual treatments (attending, hypersensitivity to light, visual fixation)
    j. Grandin's Hug Machine

Application Exercises & Project Suggestions

1. Observe a class for children with autistic children. List three communication strategies for children with autism used in the observed classroom.
2. Compare two intervention strategies used in autism. Document strengths and needs.
3. Discuss two living alternatives for adults with autism. How can parents, teachers, and community agencies help adults with autism achieve these living options.

InfoTrac® Activity Suggestions

Activity 12.1: Interventions in the area of Autism
This activity is based on an article that discusses intervention strategies in the area of autism. It reviews both effective and unproven interventions strategies.

1. Using InfoTrac®, locate and read "General Review: Autism-Part II" published by *Harvard Mental Health Letter*.

2. Name three unsubstantiated approaches that have been used in the treatment of autism.

_____

_____

_____

3. Describe the role of behavior management in intervention strategies used with children who are autistic.

_____

_____

_____

4. Describe three educational needs of children with high-functioning autism or Asperger's syndrome.

_____

_____

_____

Activity 12.2
1. Locate the article entitled "Angelman Syndrome: A Failure To Process" by Paul Lombroso.

2. Discuss three characteristics of children with Angelman syndrome.

_____

_____

_____

3. Discuss how Angelman Syndrome and Prader-Willi syndromes are alike genetically.

_____

_____

_____

InfoTrac® Article Suggestions:

- Lombroso, P. (2000). Genetics of childhood disorders: Angelman Syndrome: A failure to Process. Journal of the American Academy of Child and Adolescent Psychiatry, 39, 931.
- General Review: Autism-Part II. Harvard Mental Health Letter, 18, 1.

Key Terms

Define each:

Autism_____

pervasive developmental disorders_____

multiaxial system _____

Rett's disorder _____

childhood disintegrative disorder _____

Asperger's disorder_____

pervasive developmental disorder, not otherwise specified (PDD, NOS)_____

autistic savant_____

hyperlexia_____

tuberious sclerosis _____

Gilles de la Tourette syndrome_____

Angelman syndrome _____

Landau-Kleffner syndrome_____

Williams syndrome _____

psychogenic theories _____

psychogenic theories _____

applied behavior analysis _____

theory of mind _____

self-injurious behavior _____

pica_____

job coach _____

voice output communication aids _____

sensory integration _____

auditory integration training _____

facilitated communication _____

CHAPTER TWELVE: AUTISM
Practice Test

True or False

1. The DSM-IV-TR provides guidelines for the diagnosis of autism in children. _____

2. Facilitated communication has been proven to enhance the communication ability of children with autism. _____

3. Asperger's disorder is a form of autism. _____

4. Children with hyperlexia both read and comprehend at an early age. _____

5. Autism is frequently caused by poor parenting. _____

6. Autism is usually evident by age 3. _____

7. Autism can occur concomitantly with several other conditions. _____

8. Lovaas used an applied behavior analysis approach in working with children with autism. _____

9. Children with autism understand that others have different thoughts, plans, and perspectives from their own. _____

10. Children with autism may exhibit splinter skills during an assessment. _____

Multiple Choice

1. Characteristics of children with autism include:
   a. quantitative impairment in social interaction.
   b. quantitative impairment in communication.
   c. restrictive repetitive and stereotyped patterns of behavior.
   d. All of the above.

2. A job coach:
   a. helps train students on and off the job site.
   b. works primarily in residential facilities.
   c. is part of the supported employment concept.
   d. helps only children and adults with learning disabilities.

3. Hyperlexia is:
   a. a sub-category of mental retardation.
   b. a subcategory of autism.
   c. describes children who can read very early but have no comprehension of what has been read.
   d. a type of giftedness.

4. Stereotypic behaviors are:
   a. meaningless and repetitive.
   b. meaningful.
   c. may interfere with learning activities.
   d. are a sign of higher intelligence.

5. Possible causes of autism include:
   a. infectious diseases.
   b. insults during pregnancy
   c. abnormalities of the brain.
   d. all of the above.

6. Facilitated communication is:
   a. the same as augmentative communication.
   b. is characterized by a facilitator stabilizing the shoulder, arm, or hand to assist in typing messages.
   c. is a strategy which is used with children with autism
   d. all of the above.

7. Major characteristics of autism include:
   a. social interaction deficits
   b. communication deficits
   c. repetitive and restrictive interests
   d. savant characteristics

8. Autism occurs most frequently in:
   a. certain races
   b. certain specific cultures
   c. males
   d. females

9. Secretin is:
   a. a vitamin which helps memory
   b. a hormone which aids digestion
   c. a possible intervention in helping children with autism.
   d. has been scientifically identified as a possible cure for autism.

10. Some benefits have been noted in children with autism when:
    a. sugar is reduced
    b. insulin is increased
    c. yeast and gluten products are limited
    d. all of the above.

Matching
1. Secretin _____
2. Food allergies _____
3. echolalia _____
4. stereotypic behavior _____
5. self-injurious behavior _____
6. abnormalities of mood _____
7. pica _____

a. head banging, biting, rubbing
b. eats anything
c. gluten and yeast
d. repetitive phrases and words
e. laughs or cries for no apparent reason
f. hormone used in digestion which may help children with autism
g. repetitive and meaningless motor movements

Chapter 12: Persons with Autism Spectrum Disorders
Practice Test Answer Key

True or False
1. True
2. False. The research concerning the effectiveness of facilitated communication does not support the claims made by the proponents of this intervention strategy.
3. True
4. False. Children with hyperlexia read at an early age but do not comprehend what they have read.
5. False. Autism is not caused by poor parenting.
6. True
7. True
8. True
9. False. Children with autism do not understand that others have different thoughts, plans, and perspectives from their own.
10. True

Multiple Choice
1. A and C
2. B and C
3. A and C
4. D
5. B
6. A, B, C
7. C
8. B and C
9. C

Matching
1. f. hormone used in digestion which may help children with autism
2. c. gluten and yeast
3. d. repetitive phrases or words
4. c. repetitive and meaningless motor movements
5. a. head banging, biting, rubbing
6. e. laughs or cries for no apparent reason
7. b. eats anything

Check Your Understanding ⇨ See textbook page 527
Answer Key

1. **Describe the DSM-IV multiaxial system and the advantages in using the system to diagnose autism.**
A multiaxial system provides an accurate presentation of symptoms, associated conditions impacting autism, and the severity of the condition. It also describes a spectrum of developmental disorders associated with autism.

2. **List the medical conditions most frequently associated with autism?**
Tuberous sclerosis, Tourett's syndrome, Angelman syndrome, Landau-Kleffner syndrome, Williams syndrome, Down's syndrome have been associated with autism.

3. **Name and describe the other pervasive developmental disorders.**
Rett's syndrome occurs in females only. It is often accompanied by severe/profound mental retardation and stereotypical hand wringing or hand washing. Childhood disintegrative disorder happens after age 2 and before age 10. It is a rare condition that is often accompanied by communicational and socialization deficits as well as mental retardation and stereotypical behavior. Asperger's syndrome is more common in males. It is characterized by normal language development, socialization deficits, and stereotypical behavior. Not otherwise specified pervasive developmental disorders is characterized by common behavior and socialization deficits as well as repetitive behavior.

4. **How does autism differ from schizophrenia?**
Autism is a developmental disorder of childhood and not a psychotic disorder like schizophrenia.

5. **Prior to the acknowledgment of the genetic, neurological, and environmental causes of autism, what was the prevailing theory and treatment?**
Most believed that autism resulted from bad mothering or bad parenting. Psychotherapy was suggested for the child and the parents.

6. **Why is the prevalence of autism increasing?**
The incidence of autism is increasing because clinicians are diagnosing autism more accurately. Also more babies are surviving that would have previously died. Early intervention and special services have brought autism to the attention of the schools. Finally a different diagnostic criteria for autism was used until 1977

7. **List four of the possible causes of autism.**
Four possible causes of autism include genetic disorders, insults during pregnancy, structural abnormalities of the brain, allergies, and vitamin deficiencies.

8. **What does the term autistic savant mean?**
An autistic savant is a person with autism who has an outstanding talent or characteristic (ex. excellent immediate and long-term memory).

9. **Name the three cardinal characteristics of autism.**
The three main characteristics of autism are impairment in social interaction, impairment in communication, and repetitive and stereotypic patterns of behavior, interests and activities.

10. **Detail the advantages and disadvantages of the most common interventions used to educate individuals with autism.**

Sensory integration therapy is used today with children who have autism. This frequently results in increased social integration, greater interest in new activities, and tolerance of being touched. Pharmacology is used to control aggression, seizures, hyperactivity. It does have negative side effects. Vitamins, for some children with autism, have improved speech, increased attention span, and stabilized moods. The efficacy of vitamin therapy as been questioned. The MMR vaccination has been a suspect in the increase in autism. Some positive change in behavior has been reported as a result of the removal of yeast and gluten. However, there is limited research in this area also. Auditory integration training does seem to reduce hearing irregularities for some children. These results are not supported by any professional groups. Facilitated communication claims to assist children in the development of expressive communication. This process is not supported by professional groups. Secretin hormone has helped to bring some children with autism out of isolation. It lacks long term studies in terms of its effectiveness. Music seems to help improve cognitive, motor, and daily living skills. There is also little research in this area. Visual treatment stresses the use of specialized color or prism lenses to help in visual attending. There is little research in this area. Grandin's Hug machine produces deep pressure to calm high arousal and anxiety. It seems to be effective.

11. **How can technology be used with individuals with autism?**

Computers can be used in reading and communication. Voice output communication aids enable children with autism to choose what they would like to say. The Picture Exchange Communication System uses picture groups for skill instruction. Manual signing is often paired with pictures to increase communication.

12. **What are the key issues related to transition into adulthood for individuals with autism?**

Transition planning includes individual, family and community agencies. It uses student preferences and stresses interagency collaboration.

13. **Describe the issues that families typically have to deal with when they have a child with autism.**

Some of the issues that families of children with autism often face are confusion, frustration and anger as they seek a diagnosis for their child. They also endure a lot of stress on the family. Frequently siblings have to take care of the disabled child. The family often has little contact with non-disabled individuals.

14. **Why are auditory integration training and facilitated communication training considered controversial?**

These two interventions are controversial because they frequently claim results beyond the realm of reason. Further, there is little research to substantiate the positive intervention results.

CHAPTER THIRTEEN
PERSONS WITH PHYSICAL OR HEALTH DISABILITIES

Overview of Persons with Physical or Health Disabilities

Chapter 13 is an overview of the needs and challenges faced by individuals with physical or health disabilities. The author emphasizes the major causes of physical and health disabilities as well as providing suggestions for educational interventions for children with these disabilities.

Chapter Key Points

- Students with physical or health disabilities are labeled under four different categories under the Individuals with Disabilities Education Act. These categories are orthopedic impairments, multiple disabilities, traumatic brain injury, and other health impairments.
- Individuals with neuro-motor impairments include those with cerebral palsy, spina bifida, and spinal cord injury.
- Individuals with degenerative disease include those with muscular dystrophy.
- Functional effects of a disability include motor limitations, fatigue, endurance, pain, lack of experiences, learning issues, absenteeism, and the effects of additional impairments.
- Augmentative communication strategies are used to supplement or as an alternative to oral language.
- Assistive technology is used to maintain or increase the functional capabilities of people with disabilities.

Focus and Reflect

1. Define cerebral palsy.

_____

_____

_____

2. Discuss two strategies used in the area of augmentative communication.

_____

_____

_____

3. Discuss Duchenne muscular dystrophy.

_____

_____

_____

4. Describe what a teacher should do when a seizure occurs in the classroom.

_____

_____

_____

Chapter Guided Review

1. Physical impairments
    a. orthopedic impairments
    b. multiple disabilities
    c. traumatic brain injury
    d. other heath impairments

2. History of physical disabilities
    a. early civilization: Most cultures did not value individuals with disabilities
    b. first schools: New York, Cleveland, and Philadelphia
    c. children educated in various educational options
    d. Rehabilitation Act of 1973, Section 504
    e. Americans with Disabilities Act (1990)
    f. Education for the Handicapped Act (1975); renamed Individuals with Disabilities Education Act (1990)
    g. Technology-Related Assistance for Individuals with Disabilities Act (1988)
    h. Division between school health services and medical services established in Irving Independent School District vs. Tatro
    i. Children with physical and health problems –7.4% of the special education population

3. Causes
    a. chromosomal and genetic defects
    b. infections, drugs, chemicals, environmental agents (teratogenic agents)
    c. STORCH-Syphilis, toxoplasmosis, other, rubella, cytomegalovirus, and herpes
    d. Maternal drug abuse including alcohol use
    e. Radiation
    f. Maternal trauma from falls or car accidents
    g. Prematurity including low birth weight
    h. Asphyxia
    i. Acquired causes including trauma, child abuse, diseases, infections, environmental toxins
    j. Lead poisoning

4. Cerebral palsy
    a. Non progressive disorders of voluntary movement or posture that is caused by malfunction or damage to the brain
    b. spastic
    c. athetoid
    d. ataxic
    e. mixed
    f. hemiplegia
    g. diplegia
    h. paraplegia
    i. quadraplegia

5. Spina bifida
    a. mylomeningocele-most severe form
    b. often accompanied by hydrocephalus
    c. learning problems: mental retardation, organizational problems, language abnormalities, and visual-perceptual problems.

6. Duchenne muscular dystrophy
   a. progressive, inherited disease-weakness starting at age 3, age 10-12 in a wheelchair, death by ages 16-20 years of age
   b. issues: children know of impending death; families need a supportive environment provided by teachers and therapists

7. Juvenile rheumatoid arthritis
   a. characterized by joint stiffness, pain in joint movement, limitations in joint motion, and fever
   b. symptoms: fatigue and lack of stamina

8. Limb deficiency
   a. skeletal abnormalities including partial or total absence of arms or legs
   b. uses prosthetic devices or assistive technology

9. Traumatic brain injury
   a. temporary or permanent injury to the brain from acquired causes
   b. most cases result from car accidents
   c. effects range from no effects to severe disability
   d. recovery of abilities can last for five years

10. Seizures
    a. a sudden, temporary change in the normal function of the brain's electrical system resulting in excessive, uncontrolled electrical activity in the brain
    b. epilepsy: recurrent seizures
    c. petit mal
    d. complex partial seizures
    e. tonic/clonic: grand mal seizures

11. Asthma
    a. pulmonary disease triggered by pollen infection, air pollution, exercise, etc.

12. Diabetes
    a. caused by pancreas producing little or no insulin
    b. balance needed between medication, diet, and exercise

13. Acquired immune deficiency syndrome (AIDS)
    a. caused by virus destroying the immune system
    b. motor problems, central nervous system damage

14. Assessment of physical and health disabilities
    a. medical evaluation
    b. educational assessment
    c. psychological assessment
    d. assistive technology assessment

15. Educational considerations
    a. 46.5% educated in regular classrooms, 26.1% in separate class, and 21.2% in resource class (children with orthopedic impairments.)
    b. type of disability: stamina, accessing materials, etc.
    c. functional effects of the disability: motor limitations, fatigue, medication side effects, lack of experiences, learning issues, absenteeism, additional impairments
    d. individual and environmental factors: motivation, self-concept, social and emotional factors, self-advocacy, ineffective learning environment, and other factors

16. Meeting educational needs
    a. physical health monitoring: safe environments, school emergency procedures, infection control, and teachers trained in CPR
    b. modifications and adaptations: communication, sensory perceptual modifications, environmental arrangement, curricular modifications, assistive technology, modifications in class participation
    c. specialized instructional strategies: adapting assessment procedures, developing reliable means of response, alternative writing responses, supporting terminally ill students

17. Services for individuals with physical disability
    a. young children: issues of safety, positioning, communication, concept development, curriculum development, and augmentative communication
    b. transition into adulthood: transition plan, employment planning, college attendance, technology in the workplace, supported employment, and independent living
    c. adulthood: illness, muscle and skeletal deformities, over use of certain joints and muscles, dental and medical care needs

18. Family issues
    a. financial stress
    b. lack of leisure time
    c. exhaustion
    d. child with disabilities included as a valued and loved family member

19. Diversity
    a. context dimensions of disability
    b. environmental dimensions of disability
    c. social dimensions of disability

20. Computer assistive technology
    a. input modifications
    b. processing aids
    c. output modifications

21. Augmentative communication
    a. sign language
    b. gestures
    c. communication aids
    d. picture symbols
    e. synthetic speech

22. Positioning and seating devices
    a. frequent changes in positions
    b. prone stander
    c. side lyer
    d. corner chair

23. Mobility devices
    a. fitted wheelchairs
    b. walker
    c. power operated scooter
    d. canes
    e. crutches

24. Environmental control and assistive technology for daily living
    a. environmental control unit: allows control of telephone and electrical appliances
    b. modified toothbrushes
    c. modified hairbrushes
    d. modifications in eating and preparing of food
    e. dressing aids

25. Assistive technology for play and recreation
    a. computer games
    b. card and board games
    c. wheelchair basketball and soccer
    d. bowling modifications

26. Trends, issues, and controversies
    a. maintaining a safe, healthy environment
    b. providing specialized technology adaptations and instructional strategies
    c. appropriate assessment and curriculum

Application Exercises & Project Suggestions

1. Visit a class that serves children with physical disabilities. What curriculum and therapeutic adaptations did you notice?
2. Compare and contrast athetoid and spastic cerebral palsy? What is the specific cause of each type of cerebral palsy?
3. Discuss how you would interact with children with Duchenne muscular dystrophy. Why do you think that honesty concerning their condition is critical in developing a positive teacher-student relationship?

InfoTrac® Activity Suggestions

Activity 13.1: This article provides information concerning the causes and intervention strategies used with epilepsy.

1. Locate and read the article **"What Should I Know About Seizures"** found in *American Family Physician*.

2. What is epilepsy?

_____

_____

_____

3. How can epilepsy be treated?

_____

_____

_____

Activity 13.2: This article provides information concerning current research being conducted in the area of cerebral palsy.

1. Locate and read the article entitled **"Research in Cerebral Palsy"** by Henry Chambers found in *The Exceptional Parent*.

2. Discuss two topics in cerebral palsy that are currently being researched.

_____

_____

_____

3. Discuss two characteristics of a good study in the area of cerebral palsy.

_____

_____

_____

4. Name two organizations that advocate for individuals with cerebral palsy.

_____

_____

_____

InfoTrac® Article Suggestions

- What should I know about seizures and epilepsy? American Family Physician, 64, 105.
- Stanley, F., Blair, E., Alberman, E. (2001). Birth events and cerebral palsy: facts were not presented clearly. British Medical Journal, 322, 50.

Key Terms
Define each:

Assistive technology_____

Augmentative communication_____

Orthopedic impairments_____

Multiple disabilities_____

Traumatic brain injury_____

Other health impairments_____

Teratogens_____

Neuromotor impairments_____

Cerebral palsy_____

Spastic cerebral palsy_____

Athetoid cerebral palsy_____

Ataxic cerebral palsy_____

Hemiplegia_____

Diplegia_____

Quadriplegia_____

Tube feeding_____

Individualized health plan_____

Orthotics_____

Contractures_____

Spinal cord injuries_____

Spina bifida_____

Clean intermittent catheterization_____

Duchenne muscular dystrophy_____

Junvenile rheumatoid arthritis_____

Limb deficiency_____

Seizures_____

Epilepsy_____

Insulin-dependent diabetes_____

Acquired immune deficiency syndrome (AIDS)_____

Learned helplessness_____

Specialized instructional strategies_____

Communication breakdown_____

Transition plan_____

Supported employment_____

Job coach_____

Contextual dimensions of disability_____

Social dimensions of disability_____

Technology productivity tools_____

Information technology instructional technology_____

Word prediction program_____

Walker_____

Environmental control unit_____

Reliable means of response_____

Spread_____

CHAPTER THIRTEEN: PERSONS WITH PHYSICAL OR HEALTH DISABILITIES
Practice Test

True or False

1. Spina bifida is caused by a defect in the brain. _____

2. Diplegia is a condition in which the arms are more involved than the legs. _____

3. Spastic cerebral palsy is characterized by jerky uncoordinated movement. _____

4. The IHP (individual health plan) provides information concerning the child's specialized health services. _____

5. Duchenne muscular dystrophy is characterized by progressive muscular weakness which is terminal in nature. _____

6. The results of traumatic brain injury are quickly resolved. _____

7. Individuals usually recover fully from spinal cord injuries. _____

8. Petit mal seizures are characterized by momentary lapses of consciousness.

_____

Multiple Choice

1. Cerebral palsy is:
    a. progressive.
    b. a disease.
    c. caused by brain damage.
    d. results in motor impairment.

2. STORCH is an acronym for:
    a. diseases causing cerebral palsy.
    b. conditions resulting diabetes.
    c. conditions resulting in sickle cell anemia.
    d. conditions resulting in child abuse.

3. Spastic cerebral palsy is characterized by:
    a. uncoordinated, drunken movements.
    b. tight jerky movements.
    c. constant movements.
    d. none of the above.

4. Athetoid cerebral palsy is characterized by:
    a. uncoordinated, drunken movements.
    b. tight jerky movements.
    c. constant movements.
    d. none of the above.

5. Grand mal seizures have the following characteristics:
    a. stiff and jerky movements.
    b. individual is unconscious.
    c. individual is exhausted.
    d. all of the above.

6. In Duchenne muscular dystrophy
   a. the child recovers.
   b. the child has a normal lifespan.
   c. the child usually dies between 16-20 years of age.
   d. none of the above.

7. Supported employment has the following job options:
   a. job coach
   b. sheltered workshop
   c. group home
   d. institutional living

8. Augmentative communication is:
   a. used when the child can not speak effectively
   b. is critical to the student in making his/her wishes known
   c. often thought to slow the development of speech
   d. none of the above

9. Contractures are:
   a. type of surgery used in cerebral palsy.
   b. a type of medication used in cerebral palsy.
   c. shortened muscles that result in the inability to fully extend the joint.
   d. another name for a prone stander.

10. In paraplegia:
    a. the arms are involved.
    b. the legs are involved.
    c. both the arms and legs are involved.
    d. none of the above.

Matching

1. "Children of God" _____
2. Little's disease _____
3. grand mal seizure _____
4. mylomeningocele _____
5. environmental control unit _____
6. traumatic brain injury _____
7. augmentative communication _____
8. transition plan _____
9. assistive technology _____
10. other health impairment _____

a. injury to brain caused by an external physical force
b. the most severe form of spina bifida
c. supplementary forms of communication
d. Middle Ages view of individuals with disabilities
e. system used to increase functional capabilities
f. another name for cerebral palsy
g. limited strength and alertness affecting education
h. a plan to assist in moving into the work force
i. assistive technology used to control appliances
j. a seizure characterized by tonic/clonic movements

Chapter 13: Persons with Physical or Health Disabilities
Practice Test Answer Key

True or False
1. False. Spina bifida is caused by a defect in the neural tube.
2. True
3. True
4. True
5. True
6. False. Traumatic brain injury take children one to five years to recover.
7. False. Spinal cord injuries are usually permanent.
8. True

Multiple Choice
1. C and D
2. A
3. B
4. C
5. D
6. C
7. A
8. A and B
9. C
10. B

Matching
1. D
2. F
3. J
4. B
5. I
6. A
7. C
8. H
9. E
10. G

Check Your Understanding ⇨ **See textbook page 594**
Answer Key

1. **Which IDEA categories include students with a physical or health disability, and how are they defined?**
Orthopedic impairments include children with congenital impairments, diseases, or other causes. Multiple disabilities include children that have two or more primary disabilities that cannot be accommodated by one special education program. Traumatic brain injury includes students that have an acquired brain injury as a result of external force. Other health impairments include children that have limited alertness to the educational environment because of health problems that limit strength and vitality.

2. **What is the importance of the Supreme Court decision in Irving Independent School District vs. Tatro and Cedar Rapids Community School District vs. Garret?**
Irving Independent School District vs. Tatro established a division between school health services (performed by a nurse), which the public school is responsible for providing, and medical services (services that require a physician) which the school is not responsible for providing. Cedar Rapids Community School District vs. Garret F. required school personnel to perform specialized health-care procedures that would allow Garret to attend public school.

3. **What are the major causes of physical or health disabilities?**
The major causes of physical and health disabilities are multiple disabilities, orthopedic impairments, other health impairments, and traumatic brain injury.

4. **Explain the following conditions: cerebral palsy, spina bifida, traumatic brain injury, Duchenne muscular dystrophy, limb deficiency, seizure disorders, and AIDS.**
Cerebral palsy is a non-progressive condition which effects motor ability and is caused by malfunction or damage to the developing brain. It occurs before, during, and after birth. Spina bifida is the interruption of the development of the neural tube. It involves the spinal cord and meninges. The three types are occulta, meningocele, and mylomeningocele. Traumatic brain injury refers to temporary or permanent injury to the brain from acquired causes such as car accidents, accidental falls, and gunshot wounds. Duchenne muscular dystrophy is characterized by progressive muscle weakness from degeneration of the muscle fiber. Weakness starts to appear at age three. Children are in wheelchairs by age 10-12. Death occurs between 16 and 20 years of age. Limb deficiency is any number of skeletal abnormalities in which arms or legs are partially or totally missing. Seizure disorders are a sudden temporary change in normal functioning of the brain's electrical system as a result of excessive, uncontrolled electrical activity in the brain. AIDS is an illness that destroys the immune system leaving the person open to serious, life-threatening diseases.

5. **Explain the steps you would take if a tonic-clonic seizure occurred in your classroom.**
The teacher should stay calm, move furniture out of the way to prevent injury, loosen the child's shirt collar, put something soft under his/her head, turn student to side to allow saliva to drain out, call an ambulance for seizures lasting more than five minutes, give mouth to mouth resuscitation if breathing stops, allow student to rest, reassure the student after the seizure ends.

6. **What is an IHP?**
An IHP is an individualized health plan which provides procedures, goals, and information concerning specialized procedures for the child.

7. **How does a physical or health impairment affect school performance?**
The type of disability, functional effects, and environmental factors can interact to negatively effect the student's school performance.

8. **What does it mean to maintain a safe, healthy environment?**
Maintaining a safe, healthy environment includes having efficient evacuation plans, school emergency procedures, infection control procedures, and teachers trained in CPR and first aid.

9. **What types of modifications and adaptations may need to be used in the classroom? Include seven major areas in your discussion.**
The areas of classroom modifications needed for children with physical or health disabilities include environmental arrangement, communication, instructional and curricular modifications, assistive technology for content areas, class participation, modification of assignments and classroom tests, and sensory-perceptual modifications.

10. **Describe how communication breakdowns can occur when talking with an individual with an augmentative communication device. Describe some techniques to prevent such breakdowns from occurring.**
Some students cannot use the communication device effectively when they are learning how to use it. The teacher can ask questions with a multiple choice format being used for answers. The regular and special education teacher should note the best ways of communicating with the student.

11. **What are specialized instructional strategies and specialized expanded curriculum areas? Provide examples.**
Specialized instructional strategies include special techniques in phonics, adapting assessment procedures, alternative means for writing, and supporting ill students. Specialized expanded curriculum is specified in the child's IEP. The specialized curriculum will include adaptations for independent living, health care, social skills, vocational skills, community skills, and leisure skills.

12. **What are some stresses that occur with families who have a child with a physical or health impairment?**
The stresses include the demands of the disability and medical treatment, financial strains, lack of leisure time, routine changes and disruptions, exhaustion, and communication breakdown with family and friends. Some stresses that are different than those experienced by other families with disabled children include daily care that needs to be performed for the child, regular medical treatment, chronic illness, and degenerative conditions resulting in death.

13. **What are the major types of assistive technology in the area of physical or health disabilities?**
The major types of assistive technology are computer assistive technology, augmentative communication, positioning and seating devices, mobility devices, environmental control and assistive technology in daily living, and assistive technology for play and recreation.

14. **What is augmentative communication? Does its use interfere with speech production?**
Augmentative communication is various forms of communication used as a supplement or alternative to oral language. It includes gestures, sign language, alphabet, picture symbols, communication devices, and computers with synthetic speech. Augmentative communication enhances speech production, when possible, and is important in helping children to communicate thoughts, participate in class, and socialize.

15. **What is "spread" and how may it affect a person with a physical or health disability?**
Spread is the overgeneralization of a disability to unrelated areas. This may result in students with physical or health disabilities being placed in inappropriate curriculums and teaching them less than what they are capable.